D1339970

Towards an Igbo Metaphysics

Emmanuel M. P. Edeh, C.S.Sp.
Professor of Philosophy of Education

Loyola University Press • Chicago

Loyola University Press
3441 North Ashland Avenue
Chicago, Illinois 60657

Reprinted with due permission in Nigeria by
Our Saviour Press Ltd., 1999
84 Agbani Road/Enugwu-Ukwu Street,
Uwani, Enugu, Enugu State.

2nd reprint with due permission in the United Kingdom by
Minuteman Press, Broad Street, Banbury 2007

Acknowledgements:
    Maps of Africa and Igboland
    by William L. Nelson

Cover art:
    by J. L. Boden
    from *MMWO Society Mask*,
    Africa, Nigeria, Ibo people,
    wood, fiber, pigment. 40.7 cm. high.
    The Art Institute of Chicago.

Design by J. L. Boden

Library of Congress Cataloging in Publication Data

Edeh, Emmanuel M. P.
    Towards an Igbo Metaphysics.

Bibliography: p. 177
    1. Philosophy, Igbo (African people) 2. Igbo (African people)
1. Title.
DT515.45.133E34   1985   110'.89963   84-21788
ISBN 0-8294-0460-0
ISBN 978-2166-37-5   1999.

Dedicated to
my beloved parents
Mr. & Mrs. Edi Ani Onovo & Nwankwo Nogo
and all sons and daughters of
Akpugo in Nkanu

Contents ▨▨▨▨▨▨▨▨▨▨▨▨▨

Part Two

Toward a description of metaphysics

chapter three: The Origin, structure and purpose of the universe

chapter four: An Igbo understanding of being

Appendices

Preface

The debate whether Africa has a philosophy has in recent years given way to a much more pertinent question: What is African philosophy? This can be rephrased thus: How is African philosophy articulated and presented? Philosophy as such is all encompassing, that is, it aims at the comprehension of a whole mode or form of life. Africa is part of our global society. It has a distinct culture with healthy cultural values and meanings. True philosophy based on true human values and meaning therefore cannot but embrace Africa's unique contribution.

But Africa's contribution cannot be given a fair chance without serious efforts on the part of the African elites. These elites are born into and live African culture. It behooves them, therefore, to engage in the actual doing of African philosophy, that is, to articulate and present in a coherent manner the specific ways in which African peoples have conceived existence, beings, and Being. With this aim I have undertaken to present an African philosophy as articulated in the metaphysics of the Igbos of Nigeria in West Africa.

In carrying out this project I have been deeply encouraged by the thoughtful and gracious assistance of many persons without whom my dreams would never have materialized. DePaul University of Chicago has been generous in sponsoring my research. To this institution I owe a special debt of thanks. I am deeply indebted to the members of the department of philosophy who stimulated my inquiries and guided my efforts.

My special thanks go to Professors T. N. Munson, Gerald F. Kreyche, and R. Lechner, all of DePaul University, and I. I. Egbujie of Boston College, Massachusetts, for their suggestions and directions, and to Barbara Zak, who typed the manuscript.

In addition to those who have aided me directly in this research, others have supported me in various ways during my work. Fr. Dominic C. Carmon, pastor of St. Elizabeth Church, and Fr. Charles J. Kouba, pastor of SS. Cyril and Methodius Church, provided a congenial working environment. Mrs. Margaret D. Brennan was a generous benefactress of my seminary days, and she and her family have continued their aid with familial warmth and encouragement. My sister, Maria-Goretti Edeh, as well as Mr. Emmett King Patrick, Jr. and Mr. Francis U. Ujam, have been ongoing sources of strength.

I would like to acknowledge my indebtedness to all those whose works have been in any way helpful to me, among whom are Professor I. I. Egbujie, Dr. E. Obiechina and a host of others as my references and bibliography indicate.

Finally I wish to thank my Provincial Superiors and the members of the Holy Ghost Fathers of Nigeria East for their tolerance, patience, and understanding. They, and others too numerous to mention, have contributed to the success of this venture.

E. M. P. Edeh

General Introduction

Western philosophy began with the Greeks. Greek philosophy was formally presented by figures like Socrates, Plato, and Aristotle. Their presentations consisted primarily in attempts to develop a systematic position on the basis of philosophical speculation: a cosmology, an ontology, and the like.

For a while now there has been much talk about African philosophy (African thought). The idea of African philosophy will ever remain a figment of the imagination until it is formally presented by a people of Africa just as Western philosophy was presented by the Greeks. The aim of this study is to attempt a presentation of African philosophy by a people of Africa (the Igbos). My effort will consist of a presentation of Igbo metaphysical thought patterns.

People who have written on African philosophy are fond of making the distinction between ancient, traditional, and modern African philosophy. In this maiden work on Igbo metaphysics I will not ignore these distinctions. Yet my discussion will not be explicitly organized under these themes. My intention is to cut across them. I treat the metaphysical aspect of Igbo philosophy as it stands now. This does not mean discussing the thought-pattern of the modern Igbos as affected by Western trends of thought. Rather, the intention is to investigate the Igbo metaphysics as it is at present, that is, as the product of its past. Hence, I will present the Igbo metaphysical thought-content as the culmination of its ancient and traditional stages. What I am doing, therefore, is the contemporary metaphysics of the Igbo people with due regard to the ancient and traditional thought patterns.

The rest of this general introduction will give sketchy geographical descriptions and brief historical surveys of the continent and

1

the country where the Igbos are located, and will end with the historical background of the Igbos. All these are expected to serve as a necessary background to the understanding of the Igbo people's philosophical mentality in general and their grasp of the metaphysical questions in particular.

Africa: A Continent

As an African travels through the United States of America, he or she is at times confronted with a couple of questions, such as:

> Q.   Where are you from?
>
> A.   I am from Nigeria in West Africa.
>
> Q.   My cousin, Bill Goodman, is working in the gold mines of Johannesburg, do you know him?

What is embarrassing about the above questions is not what they literally mean, but what they imply; namely, that Africa is so small (perhaps as small as one of the fifty States that make up the United States of America) that one who is from Nigeria in West Africa should be able to know someone who has no special affiliation to him except that he is in Johannesburg, which is in South Africa.

For the benefit of our readers and those who ask such questions we shall give a brief geographical survey of Africa and the country of Nigeria as a prelude to a geographical circumscription of the Igbos. Africa is the second largest of the continents (second only to Asia).[1] It has not less than fifty countries.[2] It has an area of 11.7 million square miles, and it is located squarely across the equator, with its northern and southern extremes nearly equidistant from the equator at 37°21' North and 34°51' South respectively. Four-fifths of the area of Africa, that is about 9 million square miles, lie between the two Tropics of Cancer and Capricorn. Consequent on the geographic position of Africa, the great percentage of its vast lands enjoy the tropical climate that is generally warm and free from the violent fluctuations in temperature found, for example, in North America. "More significantly," says an American historian, Robert W. July:

> Africa's geographic position affects the pattern of rainfall which in turn has had a profound influence on African ecology and history. The latitudes adjacent to the equator north and south are covered by a blanket of low-pressure air which rises from the hot land in response to the near vertical rays of the sun. Thus is created a re-

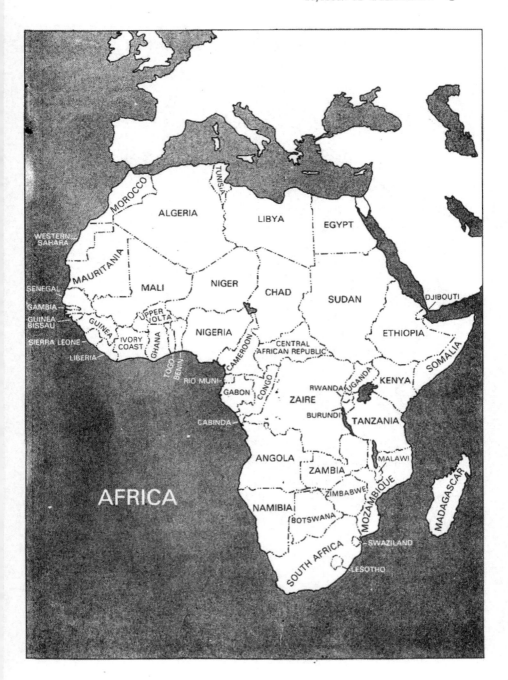

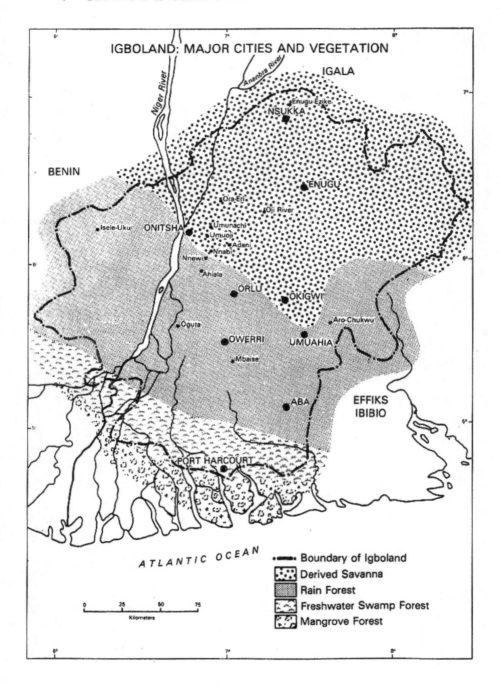

gion of heavy rainfall, and here—principally in the Congo River basin and the Guinea Coast of West Africa—is to be found the verdant rain forest capable at once of sustaining high population density and resisting the inroads of unwelcome intruders. This rich growth does not extend across the continent to East Africa, however, where wind, sea and topographical conditions limit precipitation and, hence, vegetation in that area.[3]

As one moves away north and south of the equator the rainfall gradually diminishes through the zone of the trade winds until one reaches the subtropical high-pressure belt. Here the precipitation is less than ten inches a year falling on the desert regions of Africa.

On the whole, as the result of African topography, one can say that Africa consists of a great block of ancient rock that has been little disturbed over two hundred million years, except for periodic uplift and erosion. A considerable number of plateaus[4] tilt slightly upward to the east and the south and peak with Kenya Mountain, Kilimanjaro Mountain, and the Cameroon Range. A valley beginning with the Gulf of Agaba at the head of the Red Sea runs a course of four thousand miles southwards through the Ethiopian highlands, flanks Lake Victoria east and west, finally forms the Lake Malawi depression, and terminates on the eastern coast near the Mozambique city of Beira.

The great continent is blessed with a series of major rivers whose meandering courses through much of their long passage occasionally spread out into broad, shallow basins that once held inland seas. These rivers in many places spill over the continental edge of the plateaus in waterfalls and cause rapids before emptying into the sea. A considerable means of internal transportation and communication is provided through these river systems of Africa.

If we accept the most recent conclusions of many archaeologists, we can say that Africa is historically the most senior of the five continents in the world in the sense of sustaining human life. The archaeologists believe that man's ancestors first became differentiated from primates in Africa. Authors, especially in the United States, differ in their accounts of the archaeological finds.[5] However, the gist of what they are saying is that the fossilized remains of *homo habilis* and *homo erectus*, the ancestors of man, were found in East Africa near Lake Victoria, which is nearly two million years ago. From *homo erectus* developed what is known today as *homo sapiens* (the modern man). By the time man adopted a settled life in agriculture and stock-raising some six or seven thousand years ago, the main racial types now living in Africa were there.[6]

Here it is pertinent to note that the archaeological findings mentioned above do not at all contradict the biblical account of creation. Archaeological minds work on what could have happened some millions of years ago. They try to unravel scientifically the apparent mystery surrounding the similarities that do exist between human beings and animal species. For example, archaeologists and paleontologists like L. S. B. Leakey have even gone beyond two million years to suggest that by the Miocene times a creature named *Kenyapithecus Africanus* appeared in East Africa at least twenty million years ago. While coexisting with true apes, *Kenyapithecus* possessed certain characteristics of facial bone structure and dental arrangement akin to those of modern man. This prompted Leakey to suggest that *Kenyapithecus* was a hominid, that is, man type as distinguished from the ape line of pongids. "For Leakey, therefore, it followed that the hominid family had already split from the pongids as long ago as twenty million years, and a common ancestor for man and ape must have lived in Africa in an even more remote past."[7] Of course the findings of recent genetic studies have sharply contested the chronology of Leakey's hypothesis. These studies suggest that man and the great apes of Africa may have branched off from each other as recently as four or five million years ago.

These are intelligent estimates based on the archaeological discoveries. The message of the biblical account of creation is in no way undermined. That God created all beings, man included, can never be questioned. The researches of archaeologists and paleontologists are but human efforts to deepen man's knowledge of the mysterious creative action of God. The efforts of the archaeologists and paleontologists to locate where and when man and the great apes branched off from each other could be seen as the human attempts at pinpointing the exact place where and the time when God "breathed life-giving breath [the soul] into his [man's] nostrils" (Gen. 2:7). It is difficult to locate the exact time and place of God's creation of man because God and His creative actions transcend time and place. He, as the creator, is the only one who actually knows the accurate chronology of all beings. Human beings can at best make intelligent guesses.

This brief discussion of the genesis of man in Africa will help us to understand how deep and original African philosophy typified in Igbo metaphysics is. The proper African philosophy is not borrowed from Europe, America, Asia or Australia. The results of the archaeological finds we discussed briefly above have shown that, with due respect to the biblical account of creation of man by God, man has lived in Africa from the earliest times. Hence it is not an exaggeration to say that African philosophy is as old as man.

West Africa

According to oral traditions and written records, the discoveries of the archaeologists, accounts and chronicles compiled by Arab travelers, merchants and scholars, West African history is long and varied. For our purposes we mention the highlights of the areas in West Africa. As this history shows, large cities and states have flourished in West Africa as early as the fifth century A.D. The empire of Ghana flourished as a wealthy state from the fifth to the thirteenth centuries with an established system of taxation and administration. Mali, a large state that extended from the Atlantic to the western edge of modern Nigeria conquered Ghana and held dominion from the twelfth to the fifteenth centuries. Its greatest ruler, Mansa (Emperor) Musa, was well known among the Venetian merchants. The Songhai Empire replaced Mali in the fifteenth century and became the largest empire to appear in the western Sudan.[8] However, Songhai fell to the Moroccans between 1590 and 1618.

Between the eleventh and the nineteenth centuries, the kingdom of Kanem, located to the northeast of Lake Chad, flourished with its center of political power in Bornu. The Hausa States appeared in the ninth century in the area between the Niger River and Lake Chad. They maintained economic and cultural contacts with North Africa. In the seventeenth century, a period of exceptional economic activity, trade routes across the Sahara from Tunis and Tripoli in North Africa terminated at the Hausa towns of Kano and Katsina.

The close of the eighteenth century saw the Fulani kingdom rise as a result of a religious revisal. Usuman dan Fodio, an ardent Moslem Fulani, organized a *jihad* (holy war) that by 1810 successfully replaced the old Hausa dynasties with Fulani emirs. The head of the resulting Fulani Kingdom was the Sarduana (Emperor) of Sokoto, the capital city of the empire. Today the Sarduana of Sokoto still wields a tremendous influence in northern Nigeria.

Our brief sketch of the early background history of West Africa will not be complete without some mention of the States of Guinea. Geographically the terms *Guinea* and *Sudan* are used to describe the forested area in the southern half of west Africa and the northern half, or the Savanna, respectively. Evidently states similar to those in the Sudan existed in the southern area. Their culture traits, for instance, art forms, have been traced to the Nok Society that flourished in the southern savanna between 900 B.C. and 200 A.D. The old belief that credits immigrants from the Nile Valley with founding the Guinea States has been disproved by modern studies. It is now certain that while immigrants from the Sudanic States would have infiltrated the forested areas of the southern states, there are cities in these states which have been occupied by indigenous inhabitants since time immemorial. People like the Akan, who lived in what is modern Ghana today, organized states. Also, states were organized by the Yoruba of western Nigeria. Benin, the present capital of Bendel State in modern southwestern Nigeria, was known to the Europeans from the sixteenth century on and was compared favorably with large European cities of that time. It was famous for its art in iron and bronze. Further southwest of Nigeria, the Yoruba state of Oyo controlled wide areas in West Africa. It had an early reputation for superior art in stone, bronze and iron.

Modern Nigeria

Modern Nigeria, the most powerful country (economically, militarily and in population) in Africa was established on January 1, 1914. This, of course, was the result of the amalgamation of the British Colony and Protectorate of Southern Nigeria with the British Protectorate of Northern Nigeria, all in West Africa. The country became independent of the British colonial masters in 1960. It covers an area of 356,669 square miles with a total population of approximately one hundred million. At the time of our writing, Nigeria is comprised of nineteen states united under a military government.

Modern Nigeria is made up of many ethnic groups, but the three major ones are: the Yorubas, the Hausas and the Igbos.[9] From what we have seen so far, we know that from antiquity the Yorubas have lived and organized their culture in the Southwest of Nigeria. We have also known that the Hausas have from antiquity developed and lived their culture in the northern part of Nigeria. This leaves us with the question: What of the Igbos?

The Igbos

The Igbos are a people principally located in southeastern Nigeria, West Africa. They also extend to parts of the midwestern and delta regions of Nigeria. The Igboland covers Imo, Anambra and the eastern part of Bendel states. It lies between latitude 5 to 6 degrees north, and longitude 6.1 to 8.5 degrees east. Covering an area of approximately 16,000 square miles, it has borders on the east with the Ibibio people. On the west it is bounded by Bini and Warri people. The Igbos share their northern boundary with the Idomas; and their southern boundary with the Ijaws and the Ogoni.

The river Niger, before emptying itself into the Atlantic Ocean through a network of tributaries, divides the Igboland into two unequal parts: the Western Igbos and the Eastern Igbos. The Western Igbos are only one-tenth of the total, whereas the Eastern Igbos constitute about eight-tenths. The rest of the Igbos are scattered in other parts of the world.

According to the population estimate in 1921, the Igbos numbered four million. The 1963 Nigerian census had the Igbos at ten million. But today with the total Nigerian population at around a hundred million, the Igbos are estimated to number approximately thirteen million. This shows a statistical increase of about 200 percent from 1921 to 1981. The Igbo population is unevenly distributed. The bulk of it is concentrated along the Onitsha, Orlu, Okigwi and Mbaise geographical axis, where the density is well over 2,000 persons per square mile.[10]

Apart from the river Niger, other considerably large waterways are the Anambra, the Cross, and the Imo. In the main, Igboland is low lying, with the exception of Awgu (1,287 ft.), Enugu (1,715 ft.), and Nsukka (1,315 ft.). A vegetational survey of Igboland shows that it falls into four major belts:

1. Mangrove forest, at the delta, barely touching the southern Igboland;

2. Fresh water swamp forest, covering Ahọda, Port Harcourt and Opobo areas;

3. Rain forest region, making a rugged channel from Agbor and Ọgwashi-uku, through Orlu and Owerri, down to Elele and up through Aba to Umuahia;

4. Derived savanna, covering most of the rest of the land running from northwest to northeast. This last vegetational belt includes Onitsha, Nsukka, through Enugu, down to Okigwi, Bende, Afrikpo and up to Nkalagu and Abakaliki.

Historical survey of the Igbos

On the question of the origin of the Igbos two hypotheses summarize most of the guesswork and suggestions so far put forward by Igbo enthnologists and historians. These are the Outside Origin and Ancient Origin hypotheses.

Outside origin

According to the hypothesis, the Igbo tradition of origin is traceable to an area outside the present Igboland. The majority of the exponents of this view very often point to the East as the place of Igbo origin. For example: C. R. Niven, a former colonial official in Nigeria, wrote:

> There are living today along the two great rivers of Nigeria many tribes using languages . . . (who) . . . for the most part have no traditions except the almost universal one . . . of having come from the East, from Mecca, from Egypt and elsewhere but always from the East.[11]

The Effiks, the Igbos' southeastern neighbors themselves testify to the fact that they had come from Egypt down to the banks of the Niger. From there they moved on to the locations today known as Umuahia, Bende, Abam, and later on to Arọ-chukwu, from where they finally moved to their present settlement. Even though the Effiks are not Igbos, from testimony one thing is clear: that some Nigerian people, be it the Igbos or the Effiks, could have come at one time or another from the East.

What is peculiar about the hypothesis of outside origin is that it does not suggest that all the Igbos are from the same place. In fact, from the information gathered from oral tradition, the natives who are positive about the claim of outside origin do so on the basis of their own particular kinship, not that of the entire Igbo people. The most notable claimants of the outside origin hypothesis are the Onitsha-Igbo and Arọ-chukwu Igbo.

Onitsha-Igbo: According to Leonard, it seems evident that the Onitsha-Igbo had a Bini origin.[12] N. W. Thomas in his anthropological report shows that the original Onitsha people were located some miles from Isele-Ukwu for some time before they were driven out by the forces of Benin.[13] However, Thomas's work on this issue proves only that Onitsha-Igbo people migrated from somewhere out-side Igboland but not outside Nigeria.

Arǫ-Chukwu-Igbo: Another group of the Igbos which has a strong probability of outside origin is the Arǫ-chukwu. Testifying to this, Frank Hives, a district commissioner in Nigeria, wrote in 1905:

> The Arǫs were quite a different racial type from the indigenous in-habitants of the Ibo country.[14]

He also hypothesized that, because the Arǫs were light in colour, they must have been among the people associated with the descendants of a Phoenician colony that had settled on the lower Congo in a very distant past and had intermarried with the natives. The best that can be said about Hives's view is that it represents an intelligent guess because in general the Igbos are usually lighter in colour than the neighboring ethnic groups of Nigeria. But even if Hives's view of Arǫ-chukwu outside origin were true, there would be an apparent contradiction because the Arǫs have claimed even until today that they were not from outside Igboland. According to oral tradition, Arǫ-chukwu is the oldest town in Igboland. But paradoxically, this oral claim is undermined by the text of the Ajali-Arǫ Agreement of August 17, 1911, which reads:

> Now we, the Arǫs, recognize that the land we live on and that our forefathers lived on is not our property but the property of the Ibos, the original inhabitants of the country. We, therefore, agree on behalf of ourselves and our people to pay the Ibos ... an annual nominal rental of five pounds sterling ... and we the Arǫs and Ibos fully understand the agreement we are signing.[15]

The contradiction of text, and Igboland oral tradition would require painstaking research to resolve. Since this matter relates more to history than to philosophy, I leave it to the Igbo historians.

Another striking version of the outside origin hypothesis is the suggestion of a Jewish origin. For example, Basden supports this view with reference to the similarities in marriage customs, in observance of the new moon and certain other common cultural and social functions. However, a closer inspection of these similarities shows that it has little or no claim to validity. I am led to this conclusion by the fact that if the major evidence for a Jewish origin is the cultural similarities between the two peoples, what are we to make of the fact that the same cultural similarities also exist between the Igbos and many other African peoples? On the basis of cultural similarities, can one not easily argue that it was the Jews who originally in a very distant past migrated from Africa? This contention might conceivably be buttressed by the biblical account of the Jewish exodus from Egypt. There is food for thought here, but no compelling evidence.

Ancient origin hypothesis

There is a stronger probability for the tradition that the Igbos did not migrate from outside but rather they developed independently like other indigenous African peoples. The recent archaeological finds of Professor Thursten Shaw of the Institute of African Studies at the University of Ibadan, and of Professor Hartle of the University of Nigeria at Nsukka, and the researches of Dr. Onwuejeogwu, an Igbo ethnologist, are of great importance in determining the weight of this hypothesis. Prominent among the excavations made between 1959 and 1960 by Shaw are the Igbo-Ukwu bronze objects. These have been dated around 1000 A.D. Hartle's own archaeological collections made at Bende, Afikpo, Okigwi, Awka and Nsukka, have shown that the Igbos had settled in those areas as far back as 205 A.D.[16]

Judging from the archaeological collections of Shaw and Hartle, Onwuejeogwu has suggested a strong continuity of materials between the Nri culture[17] of 580 A.D. and that of the present time. In his view the undated objects collected by Hartle could rightly be said to fill one of the gaps between 580 A.D. and the 20th century.[18] An Igbo theologian, P. O. Achebe, arguing from the results of the works of Shaw, Hartle and Onwuejeogwu, theorized that there has been a continuous occupation of igboland for at least 3,000 years. Other recent discoveries disclose the fact that the occupants of Igboland developed a civilization 1,000 years ago. This is almost half a millennium before the emergence of the kingdom of Benin[19] from which, according to the outside hypothesis, the Onitsha-Igbo are supposed to have migrated. Even if it is the case that the Onitsha-Igbos actually came from the kingdom of Benin, we cannot therefore argue an Igbo origin in Benin.

Further evidence for the improbability of the outside origin tradition can be garnered from the writings of M. C. English, a former education officer in Nigeria. Discussing the possibility of a migration from the Sahara, he maintained that when the Sahara dried up and became a desert at the end of the Stone Age, people moved from the Sahara to the north and south of Africa. But by that time Nigeria was already inhabited.[20] Stone Age implements have been discovered at different sites in Nigeria. Hence Niven concluded from this that the Igbos and other ethnic groups had settled in their lands before the movement from the Sahara.[21] Jones and Mulhall[22] likewise maintained that Igbos did not migrate from other parts of Africa. They argued for settlement in the thickly populated parts of Nri-Awka and Isuama areas for a long period. The evidence available from these sources supports the ancient origin hypothesis. Thus that the Igbos developed independently from ancient times and hence did not migrate from outside seems tenable at least until contradictory evidence presents itself.

At this point one may ask: What is the relevance of this discussion of the historical origin of the Igbos to the theme of my work, a presentation of Igbo metaphysics? My reply is that it paves the way to an understanding of the source of the Igbo metaphysical thought-pattern. If the Igbos came from another people, it is most likely that the latter exerted some influence on the former. Hence, the originality of certain metaphysical principles will be attributed, more or less, to the Igbos depending on whether or not these principles originated with the Igbos or were inherited by them from the people from whom they migrated.

The historical background of the Igbos helps us to understand the Igbo identity. When authors[23] refer to the Igbos as "a people of their own with centuries of cultural development," we understand what they mean. Ethnologically the Igbos are an ancient race. They are a unique people with specific characteristics, a people with "a copious supply of versatile common sense and the unique capacity for improvisation."[24] In the words of Forde and Jones, the Igbos are "generally held to be tolerant, ultrademocratic. . . . They dislike and suspect any form of external government and authority. They have . . . a practical, unromantic approach to life."[25] They are characterized by a hard-working, enterprising and progressive nature.

Let us sum up our geographical and historical discussion. It is evident that the Igbos inhabit a compact stretch of land. They speak a common language. To a considerable extent they share a similar social system. The Igbos are a single people. This is born out by the reality of the cultural similarities found in all sections of the people, as we shall see in detail in chapter two of this work. Surely this is not to assert an absence of cultural differences reflected in various dialects and social institutions among the different segments of the people. But these variations are not so pronounced as to influence the unity of the fundamental metaphysical principles that are basic to the way of life of all the Igbos.

"Ibo" or *"Igbo"*: The words "Ibo" and "Igbo" have each been used to refer to both a people located southeast of Nigeria and their language. The difference between these two words is that the letter "g" is lacking in "Ibo" but included in "Igbo."

"Ibo" is frequently used by Europeans and other foreign writers. Their choice of this word is prompted by either or both of the following factors: first, they do not know that the correct word is "Igbo"; second, they find the word "Igbo" more difficult to pronounce due to its compounded letters *gb* and, hence, they choose the easier way of using "Ibo."

However, it is possible to find some Igbo writers using the word "Ibo." Their reason for this could be either that they want to anglicize Igbo or that they want to make it easy for the non-Igbos to pronounce. In my own view, neither of these considerations is cogent enough to permit us to abandon the correct spelling and pronunciation of "Igbo." This view is grounded on the fact that during the extensive fieldwork I did in all parts of Igboland, I did not find even a small section of the people that uses the word "Ibo." Among the Igbos the correct word is "Igbo" not "Ibo."

Hence I would encourage all future writers and readers of Igbo to use the correct spelling and pronunciation of "Igbo" as it is used by the people. The Westerners do not change the spellings and the pronunciations of their nouns so as to make them easy for non-Westerners to use. If they do, it will be tantamount to watering down their culture. In the same vein the Igbos should not hesitate to highlight the correct spelling and pronunciation of their important nouns, for that is part of their upholding of their own culture.

The above brief discussion was found necessary to let my readers know why throughout this work we have consistently used the word "Igbo" instead of "Ibo" as may be found in some of the literature on the people we are investigating.

Review Questions

1. Explain in detail the import of this statement:
   "The idea of African philosophy will ever remain a figment of the imagination until it is formally presented by a people of Africa just as Western philosophy was presented by the Greeks."

2. Evaluate the arguments in favor of the ancient origin hypothesis.

3. What is the relevance of a discussion of the historical background to a presentation of Ibgo metaphysics?

Part One

chapter one

The Empirical Method

When one sets out to do an original work in the philosophy of a people, the first question that comes into view is that of language. Traditionally, philosophical thought and its expression are "of a piece." Greek modes of thought, for example, have found expression in, and thus contributed to the development of, the Greek language. In this work, however, there is a difference: the thinking is in the Igbo language but the writing is in English. It would be easier for the author to think in Igbo and write in English if it were simply a matter of discussing Igbo metaphysics. But this is not the case. The aim of this work is not merely to discuss Igbo metaphysics but actually to engage in it, to do it, that is, with an Igbo consciousness. For this reason we are concerned with the question of methodology which entails two principal considerations:

    a.   field work
    b.   method of articulation

Field work

I undertook field work in two stages. The first was preliminary, during the period 1974–76, among the Nkanu people, a section of the Igbos. This was a theological-liturgical investigation, a project I initiated and completed under the direction of I. P. Anozie, former professor of Liturgy, Non-Christian Religions and Fundamental Theology at Bigard Memorial Seminary, Enugu, Nigeria. The project entailed thorough research into the people's respect for their ancestors and their traditional rites. I held numerous interviews with reliable and experienced elders of Nkanu. Questionnaires on their religious experience were used. About three hundred informants were asked the same questions. For convenience and lack of space I have chosen to present here only few informants, to show the type of empirical research involved. Eleven questions were asked each of the three different informants from three different towns located in different sections of the area under investigation. The constants are the questions. While the independent variables are the dialects, towns and ages of the informants, the dependent variables are the answers they give. As we study these answers we are able to pick out the concepts and the ideas that they highlight. These concepts and ideas will constitute the objects of our analysis in the second part of this study.

One of the things that gave me a clue to the possibility of a successful philosophical investigation into the Igbo people's way of life was my findings on the Nkanu idea of the world of the ancestors:

> Underlying the rituals observed for every individual ancestor is the emphasis on the continuation of life after death. The fact that the dead are at times seen in dreams and also the testimony of 'dibias' serve as proofs of the continual existence of those who have left this world. The funeral rites have the express intention of helping the deceased (to) reach the happy spiritland.[1]

From discoveries such as these I gained a deeper insight into the everyday activities—religious, social and above all traditional—of the Igbos. I became convinced that the proverb which says "There can be no smoke without fire," could conveniently be applied to the rites, rituals, customary observances and traditional idiosyncracies of the Igbos in this sense: there can be none of these without a philosophy that serves as its substratum.

Empirical Research
on the Nkanu Ancestor Worship
and Traditional Rites (1973–74)

Name[2]	Age	Town	Occupation	Religion
Nwokolo Njoku	97 years	Nkerefi	Farming	Traditional
Nweke Asu	86 years	Amauzam	Farming	Traditional
Ani Nwede Onovo	70 years	Amagunze	Farming	Traditional

Q. 1.   Suppose your people are in need of some favors, to whom do they pray for help?

Njoku:
1. Ani
2. Chukwu[3]
3. Ancestor
4. Aniobu Imuhu

Asu:
1. Ani Obunagu
2. Nneche ngene
3. Igwe k' ani
4. Agbalumuanyanwu[4]

Onovo:
A. Ancestors
2. Ani-land goddess
3. Various juju cults
4. Chineke[5]

Comment: These are the names of superhuman powers whom the Igbos invoke in prayer.

Q. 2.   Of all the superpowers that you invoke in prayers, does any come to your aid more than your ancestors (yes or no) Name that one.

Njoku: Yes. Ani.

Asu: Yes. Agbalumuanyanwu.

Onovo: It is difficult to say who comes to one's aid more than the others.

Q. 3.	Why are the ancestors usually buried either during morning period or evening period?
Njoku:	It is that they may rest in peace. It is believed that morning and evening are peaceful and anybody buried at those periods will equally be peaceful. He will not worry those relations who are living.
Asu:	If he has somebody he will be buried in the morning but if none he will be buried in the evening.
Onovo:	Ancestors are not buried only at that time—elderly people are buried anytime. But young people are not buried in the noonday because it's believed their ghosts may attack people.
Comment:	From these answers one gets the idea that the dead can have something to do with their families in the land of the living.
Q. 4.	Why are the ancestors buried in the homestead where they died and not in a common burial ground?
Njoku:	Because they are believed to be the guardians of the family. They are expected to look after the family as they had been doing when they were living.
Asu:	(No answer)
Onovo:	The ancestor is believed to live a normal life even after death and to bury him in the homestead is to allow him to continue living among his loved ones.
Comment:	Here is a strong indication that for the Igbos there are communications between the visible world and the invisible world. Also from these

answers we get a clue to the relationship between the living and the dead, the community
of being in the visible world and that in the
world of the unseen.

Q. 5.   Why do your people throw some food or wine
on the ground before eating or drinking?

Njoku: A sort of prayer to our ancestors to come and
eat with us.

A wine-tapper on coming down from the palm
tree in the morning usually pours some wine
on the ground. This is a libation to the
ancestors and to Ani as a sort of prayer.

Asu: We first of all offer to our ancestors and our
gods. A wine-tapper on coming down from the
palm tree in the morning usually pours some
wine on the ground. He offers this to the
ancestors and the gods and also for security.

Onovo: A wine-tapper on coming down from the palm
tree in the morning pours some wine on the
ground as an offering to Ani (land goddess) who
is the special patron of tappers and farmers.

Comment: The expression "to come and eat with us"
gives the impression that beings in the invisible world perform acts like those in the visible
world. This will help us to understand the Igbo
theory of duality in chapter three.

Q. 6.   Does death affect any change in the character
of the dead? A man wicked, cunning etc. in his
lifetime, will he continue to be wicked, cunning etc. in the spirit world?

Njoku: Yes, but not always so especially to his family.

Asu: No, because during his next coming, he will
change (dika ino uwa) the person won't be cunning or wicked again.

Onovo:	Yes, it is believed that the spirit of a wicked man is kind and that of a kind man wicked indeed—so the other way round.
Q. 7.	In what ways do the ancestors make themselves seen and felt in the family?
Njoku:	By protecting them from evils. By bringing about richness in the family. By reincarnating other young children in the family or to their sons and daughters.
Asu:	Sometimes they reincarnate in their families.
Onovo:	Through dreams, and most prominently through fortune tellers.
Comment:	What is indicated here is that there must be a place from where the dead stay and from where they can communicate with their families here on earth.
Q. 8.	How are the spirits of dead children, unmarried boy or girl regarded?
Njoku:	Bad spirits.
	Since they have nothing on earth, no son or daughter, they go about looking for lives to destroy.
Asu:	They are regarded as unclean.
	The reason is: they have died a bad death and left no achievement for their clan.
Onovo:	They are supposed to have died untimely and nobody bothers about them.
	The reason is: the parents at times regard them as "Ogbanje's" who have come to punish them. They are normally despised.

Comment:	The informants' responses here give us a clue to the Igbo idea of the origin of bad spirits whom we shall discuss in chapter four as the cause of evil.
Q. 9.	Why do your people name their children after their ancestors?
Njoku:	To keep the name of their ancestor going.
Asu:	The reason is that their names might not be forgotten (echiechi).
Onovo:	This is a form of respect and in the hope that the ancestors will take care of the child.
Comment:	These responses point to the fact that among the Igbos names carry some meaning and history behind them.
Q. 10.	Do the ancestors intervene to enforce the ethics of culture among their kinsmen on earth?
Njoku:	Yes. They do this by harassing either the eldest living member of the family or by dreams or through the work of the dibie.
Asu:	No reply.
Onovo:	Yes. They do this by punishing those who violated prescriptions of Omenani.
Comment:	Omenani is the Igbo deeper understanding of the English concept of tradition. This will be treated in detail in chapter two.
Q. 11.	Give an eyewitness account of Igo-ini[6] in your family or kindred.
Njoku:	The officiating person begins by pouring some wine on the tomb of the ancestor saying:

Nnamu nwuru mmanya, :	Let my father drink wine,
Ndichie nwuru mmanya	Let the ancients drink wine,
Ndi mma, onu di mma,	Let the well-meaning un-
Paru mmanya nwua.	seen beings, whose lips proclaim the good, take some wine to drink.
Jidenu mu na ndi be :	Protect my life and
mu ndu.	those of my household people.
Jidekwasi ndi kwere :	Also protect the lives
nkem ndu na ndi nine	of all those who do
onu di mma.	accept me and all those who speak good of others.
Ibe anyi na obu ndu. :	My brethren it is life that we want.

Everybody participating in the ritual responds with Iyaa (Amen).

At this juncture the celebrant (normally the eldest male in the family) slaughters the animals being used in the sacrifice.

The ritual ends with a feast for all the participants.

Asu: No response.

Onovo: The ceremony begins at noon. The Onye Izi takes the kola nuts and wine, and with them offers prayers to the departed father whose death is being commemorated.
He recites some incantations and the people present respond in affirmation. Then comes the pick of the ceremony, that is, the slaughtering of the livestock provided for the occasion. Feasting and dancing last until evening when

all the people in attendance retire to their homes.

Comment: "Onye Izi" is normally the eldest male in an extended family or kindred. It is interesting to note that in this ritual the entire community of being is involved—the unseen beings (ndi mma) and the living beings. Here is an indication of the Igbo idea of the community of being. This will be treated in greater detail in this study.

The second stage of my field work was undertaken in 1980 when I set out explicitly to investigate Igbo metaphysics. This was accomplished in three ways: first, I spent much time organizing an appropriate questionnaire, principally by undertaking personal interviews with people of all ranks in different sections of Igboland. This gave me the opportunity to observe the people, dialogue with them, and so feel at one with the people. This feeling I found indispensable for probing the philosophical mentality of a people whose thought patterns have not been formally articulated. The following shows the empirical method employed at this stage.

Empirical Research on Igbo Metaphysics Conducted in 1980

Hundreds of research questionnaires of various types were utilized in my field work. Here only samples of types can be included. These represent the ideas of a cross section of the Igbos ranging from the traditional illiterates to the educated priests and university professors.

Note that the omission of any of the responses of my informants in the samples does not show that those responses were of less importance than those included. All the responses have been carefully studied and each and every one of them has contributed immensely to this work.

Questionnaire Type A

Personal Data on Informant:

Name: MAZI EDE OJE
Age: Over 100 years, oldest man in Ubogu (Akpugo)
Occupation: Nze (A traditional elder)
Part of Igboland   UBOGU in Akpugo, Nkanu

An interview with a person of his age was not as straightforward as
that with a younger person. No ready-made questions could be used,
for such would be fruitless as they would not allow him to open up
the traditional wisdom of which he is an embodiment. I had several
days of fruitful discussions with him. My method was to follow him
in whatever direction he wanted to go. Here I give only a few of the
pertinent ones.

Q. 1.

Why do you always want
to sit on the oche ndi nse
(smooth-topped, stool-like
piece of wood that had
every sign of having sur-
vived through many generations) before answering my
questions?

A.   Nwam, ajuju gi gbasalu :
omenani n'ebe omiliemi
Yabu, kam wee zata ya
ofuma odi mkpa nam ga
anolu n'oche ndi Nze, kam
n'ekwu onu fa n'ekwu onu
fa n'ekwu uche fa. Oburo
n'ike akam, obu omenani.

My son, your questions are
concerned with tradition in
its depth. So that I may be
able to answer well, it is
necessary that I sit on the
stool of the representatives
of the dead, to be able to
speak their mouth, to
speak their mind; it is not
of my own authority, it is
the tradition.

Q. 2.   Kedu ife melu oche nze :
a ji di?

What made this stool of
the representatives of the
dead to be?

A. Nwam, ik'asi: Kowalu m : My son you should reframe
ife nine kpatulu oche Nze   the question thus: Explain
a ji di.   to me all that contributed
                               to making this stool.

Comment: I then reframed the question as he directed.

A. Ife melu ochea ji di bu ife : What made this stool to be
kpatalu ojiri bulu ife obu.   is that which is responsible
                                   for its being what it is.

Fa di uzo ife ano na eme : There are four groups of
kaife obuna bulu ife obu.   things that make anything
                              be what it is.

Nke mbu, ife ana afu   First, that which is visible
anya we ike imetu aka.   and can be touched.

Comment: At this juncture he pulled out the stool from under
him, touched all parts of it showing that all the visible components of the object come under this first group of things
that make the stool what it is. He then continued:

A. Nke ibua, nke zolu ezo, : Second, that which is hid-
obu odina ife na muo. Obu   den. It is that which is in
ife m ji malu na ife a bu   the object in an invisible
oche ndi Nze.   manner. It is that by which
                                 I know this is the stool of
                                 the representatives of the
                                 dead.

Comment: Then I wanted to know how that second thing comes
together with the first. He said that prior to the process of
the wood taking shape it has now and carrying the smeared
blood and other traditional decorations, the invisible was
not in it. But as soon as the wood (material object) gained the
shape, hardness, smoothness, size and other properties, as
soon as the whole stuff could be defined as what it is, namely
as "oche ndi Nze" (stool of the representatives of the dead),
the first (visible) and the second (invisible) have met.

He still proceeded to give the third and the fourth:

A.   Nke ato, onye nka, onyẹ : Third, the artisan who used
ji osisi na ife ndi ozo wee   wood and other materials
luta oche a.   to make this stool.

Nke ano, ife kpatalu eji : Fourth, the thing that
lua oche ndi Nze a. Ya bu   brought about why this
ulu obalu, ife melu ife ji di.   stool of the representatives
Nkea bu nke kachasi mkpa   of the dead was built. That
n' ime ife inoa.   is, of what value it is, the
reason why a thing is. This
is the most important of
the four.

Comment: From these answers it is clear that in Igbo thought there
are four things that are involved in the process of the coming-
to-be of any sensible object:

1. Ife ana afu anya na : The visible and tangible
   emetu aka
2. Nke zolu ozo : The hidden (invisible)
3. Onye nka : The artisan
4. Ife kpatalu : The purpose.

Q. 3.   Gini bu ife-di : What is being?

A.   Ife-di bu ife-di. : Being is being.

Q. 4.   Gini di?   What is?

A.   Ife nine bu ife-di.   All things are beings.

Q. 5.   Kedu k'isi malu na ife di? : How do you know that beings are?

A.   Amalum nkea maka na : I know this because human
madu di, maka n' anyi di.   beings are, we (human beings) are.

Q. 6.　Kedu uzo isi ama ife bu　:　How do you know what it
　　　　n'ife di?　　　　　　　　　is that beings are?

A.　Obu sita na ima ife bu　:　It is by knowing what it is
　　madu (mma-di)　　　　　that man is.

Questionnaire Type B

Personal Data on Informant:

Name:　SYLVESTER EZE
Age:　45 years
Occupation:　Priest
Part of Igboland:　NSUKKA

Q. 1.　Do the Igbos have a metaphysics?

A.　Yes.

Q. 2.　Whom do you think are pioneers in this field?

A.　Our ancestors.

Q. 3.　How has it been handed down since its inception?

A.　Orally.

Q. 4.　To what extent has it been systematically articulated?

A.　According to circumstances.

Q. 5.　Briefly state what this philosophy deals with.

A.　It deals with the realities of life not pure rationalization.

Q. 6.   Name some key concepts in Igbo metaphysics.

A.   Ife, Onye, Chukwu, Chineke, Uwa, Muo, Chi.

Q. 7.   Give some metaphysical expressions.

A.   Onye na chi ya,
Adeghi ako ikpe,
Uwa-a aburo ebe obibi,
Omume ka okwu.

Q. 8.   What are the Igbo ways of explicating these terms:

Q.	A.
Being:	Ode, Odede (there is, being)
Logos:	Okwu Onu (talk)
Logic:	Ekpeka, akoka (discussing)
Spirit:	Muo
Matter:	Ihe, Ife
Time:	Oge
Temporality:	Nwantiti
The World (Welt):	Uwa
Umwelt:	Uwa gbara Okirikiri
Science:	Imu ihe/ife
Philosophy:	Ihe kpatara ihe ife

Q. 9. What names designate the Supreme Being?

A. Chukwu, Chineke, Chidiokike, Omacha, Osebuluwa, Olisa. . . .

Q. 10. What are the different attributes of the Supreme Being?

A. Onye vu uzo ma okpe azu,
Onye okike,
Ozulu mba onu, etc.

Q. 11. Give some hint to the controversial problem of soul-body unity in Igbo philosophical thought.

A. It can concern reincarnation or witchcraft. I am not sure.

Q. 12. What major cultural and religious ceremonies of the Igbos bring out their philosophical thought implicit in their attitudes towards soul and body in man.

A. Burial, ancestor worship, Orinachi ceremony, Igu Ogbo.

Q. 13. What similarities and dissimilarities are there between Igbo and early Greek ideas of the soul?

A. Similarities: Soul exists and continues after death.
Dissimilarity: Soul exists outside the body.

Q. 14. What in your view is the one question underlying Igbo metaphysical thoughts?

A. Kedu ife bu na adi. (What does it mean that there is).

Questionnaire Type C

Personal Data on Informant:

Name: MAZI EDE ANI ONOVO
Age: 75 years
Occupation: retired counsellor,
          kindred leader.
Part of Igboland: ONUOGBA OGBANYI in Akpugo, Nkanu.

Q. 1.   Onye bu Chi-ukwu   :.   Who is Big-Chi?

A.   Chi-ukwu bu "ndi Muo"   Big-Chi is the "unseen"
        nwe ife nine, Okike kelu   who possesses all beings,
        ife, Onye nwe ndi muo na   the creator who creates be-
        ndi mma-du.   ing, who possesses the un-
                                        seen and human beings.

Q. 2.   Chi-ukwu odi ezie?   :   Does Big-Chi really exist?

A.   Chi-ukwu di ezie?   :   Big-Chi really exist (is).

Q. 3.   Kedu ka isiri malu na   :   How do you know that
        Chi-ukwu di?   Chi-ukwu is?

A.   Nkea nwolu ewu n'   :   This is obvious even to
        okuko anya. Asi na Chi-   goats and fowls. If it is said
        ukwu adiro, Ife agaghi adi.   that there is no Chi-ukwu,
                                        then being would not be.
                                        Nothing would exist.

        Asi na Chi-ukwu adiro,   :   If it is said that Chi-ukwu
        ndi Igbo agaghi na aza Chi-   does not exist, the Igbos
        ukwu-di.   would not be answering
                                        Big Chi exists as a name.

        Asi na Chi-ukwu adiro   :   If it is that Chi-ukwu does
        ndu agaghi adi.   not exist, there would be
                                        no life.

Chi-ukwu diri adi, Odifu, :	Chi-ukwu was existing, he
Oga na adilili.	is still existing, he will
	continue to exist.

Nna nna anyi fa kwulu :	Our great grand ancestors
ya. Obu etua ka Ife is di.	said it. That is how reality
	is.

Obviously in the above responses my informant has affirmed that the existence of Chi-ukwu is so obvious that the question of his demonstrability does not arise. However, a detailed scrutiny of his answers reveals some clue to the possible ways of arriving at the existence of Chi-ukwu:
1.   Existence of things of nature,
2.   Igbo nomenclature,
3.   Igbo concept of Chi,
4.   Igbo idea of life and death.

Questionnaire Type D

Personal Data on Informant:

Name: DR. AZUKA A. DIKE
Age:
Occupation: Senior Lecturer,
              Department of Sociology
              and Anthropology,
              University of Nigeria, Nsukka.
Part of Igboland: AWKA

Q. 1.   In your opinion, is Igbo way of thinking distinguished from the ways of thinking of other ethnic groups in Nigeria, and why?

A.   Yes. This is because the Igboman's upbringing and background force him to see himself as distinct from all other peoples of Nigeria.

Q. 2.   What do you think is the philosophy behind our special regard for the ancestors?

A.   Implicit in our special respect for those who lived before us is our acknowledgment that they have accumulated experience and for us experience exceeds everything. Also implicit here is our idea that the dead are not really dead. There is hardly any distinction between those living and the dead. The presence of the latter is equally felt as that of the former.

Q. 3.   Who according to the Igbos is the source of all being?

A.   This is the one whom the Igbos worship as the Supreme God and call Chukwu-Abiam. Among the Aros [a section of the Igbos] the name Chukwu, the highest Chi, is a shrine where one goes and never returns. Hence there is a saying in Igbo language:

> Nwa Aro eweghi ike igwa onye
> Aro na Chukwu cholu ya
>
> (An Aro person cannot tell a fellow
> Aro man or woman that Chukwu wants him or her).

Comment: This saying is an indication of the Igbo belief that God alone has the right of life and death of all human beings.

Q. 4.   What does the Igbo expression Owetalu oji wetal u ndu [He who brings kola brings life] indicate as it is used when a host presents a piece of kola nut to a guest?

A.   Note that this expression does not really refer to the human being who gave you a piece of kola nut. It refers rather to the creator of the kola nut. It is symbolically indicating that whoever created that kola nut is the author or source of life.

Q. 5.   Would you briefly show how life is regarded among the Igbos?

A.   During the last Biafran war there was an adage among

the Igbo soldiers: "That he who lives to fight again is a greater soldier." So one does not go into battle to die. This is a little indication that life is regarded as very precious among the Igbos. Life, especially human life, is that which only Chineke can give.

Among the Igbos, murder is the most serious sin. Murder, whether accidentally or intentionally committed, is regarded as murder insofar as life is lost. In the olden days a man who mistakenly killed a child in the bush would first run away from his village and then inform his relatives and those of the victim. The community would come together and take serious steps to make sure that such can never happen again. If they found that the accident was due to carelessness and could have been avoided, they would make sure that the culprit paid for it with his own life. If it was very clear that it was an accident that could not have been prevented or forestalled, they might not kill the offender but cows provided by him must be killed to perform what the Igbos call ikpo ochu (making up for the murder). Even today in Igboland if you, while driving, knock somebody down dead, the people around the scene must make sure that they kill you on the spot. This to some cultures may seem odd but such practice has proven to be very effective in minimizing, if not eliminating entirely, serious crimes (involving human life) among the Igbos. It makes the would-be criminals know that they cannot play with human lives and get away free.

Human life is good because it is from God. Hence the Igbo name for man is mmadi, that is, "the good that is." Whatever is good is so because of Chineke, the source of all being.

Q. 6.   In your opinion what would you say is the biggest problem in Igbo metaphysics and why?

A.   I think it should be the problem of freedom and determinism. This is because from the Igbo way of life, daily activities and manner of thinking one can deduce that God comes into man's life in every thing, every activity and so on. A traditional Igbo believes that nothing he does can become a success without the hand of God coming into it. This can be interpreted as God predetermining and directing the activities of creatures and hence raising the problem of freedom and determinism.

Questionnaire Type E

Name: MR. BENEDICT C. EMEJURU
Age: 54 years
Occupation: School Teacher
Part of Igboland: IHIALA

Q. 1.   What is the importance of proverbs in the Igbo language?

A.   The Igbos say: Ilu bu mmanu eji esuru okwu [proverb is the oil with which speech is eaten]. This shows that for the Igbos proverbs contribute immensely to the effectiveness of speech.

Q. 2.   How are Igbo proverbs grouped?

A.   There are various strata of Igbo proverbs. Some of these are:

1.   Proverbs used in the analysis of truth and sincerity, for example:
Eziokwu bu ndu.   :   Truth is life.

2.   Proverbs depicting wisdom and foolishness, for example;
Oke mmadu   :   Size does not deter-
abugh oke okwu.   mine the amount of wisdom.

3.   Proverbs on cause and effect, for example:
Awo a dagh agba   :   Nothing happens
oso efifie na nkiti.   without a cause.

4. Proverbs that show normality in the order of things in nature, for instance:

I bu adagh :	Things have their
ebugide isi	natural order to
	follow.

5. Proverbs on good and evil, for instance:

Udo adagh adi :	Peace is incompat-
ebe ajo uche di.	ible with evil
	thought.

Q. 3. Can the Igbo concept of "Ife" be used to designate human and suprahuman beings?

A. "Ife," as we know, primarily refers to inanimate things. But I think that it can also be used in an extended way to include human and suprahuman beings.

Q. 4. How can you show this?

A. O.K. Let me ask you the following questions:

Q. Kedu ife melu :	What thing made
njo n' uwa?	evil in the world?
	Or, What is the
	root of all evils in
	the world?

| A. Ego.   : | Money. |

| Q. Kedu ife melu   : | What thing made |
| Ego? | money? |

| A. Madu.   : | Man or human |
| | beings. |

Comment: In the first question "ife" refers to an inanimate entity, while "ife" in the second question refers to the human.

The second way in which I investigated Igbo metaphysics in the second stage of my field work was holding private discussions on my points of investigation with Igbo intellectuals. This method, which I found very useful, took me to the universities and institutions of higher learning in Igboland and other parts of Nigeria. While pursuing this I was fortunate to come into contact with Professor J. B. Schyler, S.J., head of the Department of Sociology at the University of Lagos. This scholar has spent his life studying the social philosophy of Africans, with particular reference to the Nigerian people.

From him I received the suggestion which became the third way of investigation in the second stage of my field work, to consult the library of San Paolo di Apostolo in Rome. This library offered me the works of Igbo scholars principally on religious and theological themes of our culture. I returned to the United States with these findings and visited the Ann Arbor Microfilm International Center at the University of Michigan. There I was able to consult dissertations written by students from Nigeria and other countries on Africa.

Method of articulation

My fieldwork and library research indicated that no serious work had been done in Igbo metaphysics. As a consequence I have undertaken here a work that is principally analytic and interpretative. I use the term *analysis* in its root meaning of breaking through the thought-content of the language, culture and some aspects of the socio-religious practices of the Igbos in a quest for the metaphysical ground supporting them. As we analyse we interpret, that is, we try to find some deeper meaning in the objects of our analysis.

Why did I choose this method of analysis and interpretation? Unlike the writers on Igbo religion, who can consult much literature, I found nothing that has been written on our subject. I hope that through an analysis of the data gathered from our research questionnaires, we can gain some insight into Igbo thought. Spoken Igbo —the names, idioms, proverbs, songs, and stories—and culture and religious practices of the Igbo people are the instruments of the investigation.

It is true that our Igbo ancestors left us no writings. But from them we have a legacy of stories, proverbs, and traditional sayings, orally transmitted from generation to generation.

Even now when Igbo literature is steadily gaining attention, contemporary Igbo authors rely very much on these stories, proverbs, and sayings for their novels. Thus in this investigation we shall capitalize not so much on written documents as on the spoken language.

Understandably, I have spared no effort in carrying out extensive field work among the Igbos. The results of our research question-naires can provide us with the firsthand information necessary to guarantee the originality and authenticity of this work.

Even the translation of ordinary literature from one language into another entails the risk of distorting the original meaning. The danger becomes ominous when we try to express in a language a philosophy done in a different language. English, as we know, is basically a Germanic language that received a powerful impact from the Normans. English, accordingly, is not without its affinities to French, and its vocabulary is rich in Latin and Greek roots.

The Igbo language, by contrast, lacks this kind of checkered background. The word *Igbo*, as it was used especially during the co-lonial days, conveyed the idea of *not English*. The expression *Igbo made* even today means *not English made*: a negative way of put-ting things that alerts us to the difficulty of using English to express our doing of Igbo metaphysics. The method of writing here will therefore include linguistic analysis and interpretation. Every effort will be made to write in English. But where there is a compelling need to express ourselves in Igbo, we shall do so, hoping that we can provide a clue to this understanding.

In the course of our investigation relevant elements of Igbo culture will be discussed. An analysis of the component parts or the peculiarities of an element of culture has the purpose of searching for deeper insights into metaphysical bases. It is the interpretative reading of the elements of Igbo culture that will reveal what is distinctively Igbo as distinguished from similar elements in kin-dred, African cultures.

A consideration of Igbo religious practices will be undertaken through the same method of analysis accompanied by an interpre-tative reading. A discussion of some relevant parts of Igbo religious practice does not mean that we lose sight of the fact that we are do-ing metaphysics, not theology. To inquire metaphysically into the way of life of the Igbos by avoiding the religious aspect of their life and hoping to come to an objective result is not possible. Studies of Igbo anthropology, culture and socio-religious life have rightly re-vealed that religion is at the heart of an Igbo man or woman. That the Igbo thinks religiously, eats religiously and sleeps religiously was correctly observed by early writers on the Igbo socio-religious mentality. Our point of interest here is this: since religion is in-grained in the being of the Igbos, it is appropriate that even in our quest for deeper understanding of the Igbo metaphysical domain of thought, we explore and utilize aspects of Igbo religious life and practice which are relevant to this investigation. The method again will be initially analytic, leading up to the discovery of the metaphysical foundation as the basis of the Igbo special attraction to religion.

We have repeated that the method to be used throughout this study is analytic and interpretative. This method is required by the original nature of the work; it is a pioneer attempt. Every pioneer work lacks a legacy of literary forms from which to draw. Consequently, one must cast one's net more broadly. Language, religious practices—culture in its broadest sense—are the data which we must investigate. It must be made clear, however, that these are not the goals but the tools for our investigation. Our interest is in the metaphysical thought of the Igbos which an analysis of their language and other elements of their culture can give us. Our interpretation leads us to the metaphysical plane, the ultimate springboard, the final source of action of the Igbos' way of life.

Finally, it is pertinent to note that our interpretation will be both theoretically and practically oriented: theoretically, because as a philosophical investigation the work is principally a quest for pure understanding; practically, because we shall survey the results of our investigation with a view to the interplay between thought and action. It behooves modern philosophical endeavor to aim not only at theoretical achievements but also at practical results. This, as we hope to show, is important in the question of Igbo metaphysics.

The Igbos, like other African peoples, are undergoing a process of modernization. This phenomenon involves changes in both the physical environment and in the mental outlook of the people. These changes are expressed in the rhythm of their way of life. This probe into Igbo metaphysics must take cognizance of these ongoing movements towards modernization. Hence, in our final section, we shall turn our attention to the practical results of our analysis and interpretation of the Igbos' idea of being.

Review Questions

1. "The aim of this work is not merely to discuss Igbo metaphysics but actually to engage in it, to do it, that is, with an Igbo consciousness." In the light of this statement provide a brief evaluation of the author's methodology.

2. Why is the method of analysis and interpretation pertinent in this study?

3. In what sense does the author use the term *analysis*. What is his justification for this?

4. Highlight the key problems encountered in the research and how they were dealt with.
5. Distinguish between the goals and the tools for this investigation.

6. Why would the interpretation involved in this study be both theoretically and practically oriented?

chapter two

The Igbo language, culture, and socio-religious milieu

The two main avenues to the thought-content of any people are its language and culture. In fact, the philosophy of a people can be stated as the underlying principles of the people's way of life as expressed in language and culture. Realizing their importance, in this chapter I am treating them as a way into Igbo metaphysics. It is through language and culture that Igbo metaphysics, or any African philosophy for that matter, is preserved and transmitted. As a consequence, in this study I shall endeavor to extract elements of metaphysics from these sources and particularly from certain Igbo religious practices.

Igbo language

The language of the Igbos is Igbo. It is a tonal language in which both grammar and speech tones play an essential role. The stress on syllables of a word, regardless of whether they are high, intermediate or low, is determinative of meaning. Thus many words that have the same orthography do not have the same tone. For example:

	àziza	means	answer, reply
while	aziza	means	brush, small broom
	àmuma	means	prophecy
while	àmùmà	means	lightning
	ama	means	space
while	àmà	means	witness

45

and	amà	means	measure
and	amà	means	distinguishing mark
	ọ̀gọ̀	means	kindness
while	ọgọ	means	in-law

Another characteristic of the Igbo language is that it has a number of dialects. The dialect of the Igbos west of the Niger is different from that of those in and around Onitsha. The dialect of the Nsukka people differs from that of Abakaliki and even Enugu. The Owerri dialect differs from even that of those nearest to them, Umuahia and Delta Igbos. But these can be regrouped under two main dialects: Onitsha and Owerri. Central to all the dialects is the official orthography adopted in 1961.[1]

The multiplicity of dialects in the Igbo language is not a unique phenomenon. In English as well as in some of the major languages of the world, such is the case. Cambridge and Oxford English are different in tone, pronunciation, speed, sometimes even in spelling, from American English.

Igbo oral usage

At the present stage of the development of the Igbo, oral tradition occupies a prominent place. Accompanying the oral is a growing literary tradition. In our discussion of language, oral tradition will be our central focus, with pertinent references to the literary forms currently in existence. The literary forms are to be found in the works of the novelists, such as Chinua Achebe, Cyprian Ekwensi, F. C. Ogbalu, and in those of a well-known Igbo writer, E. Obiechina.

Among the Igbos the ties of blood and community are very strong. Social communication and interaction are on a personal level, usually face to face. In local communities the spoken word is used as a means of establishing harmony and friendly relations between parties. A sense of integration, community solidarity and sympathetic relatedness are thus established, strengthened and fostered.

The Igbos place a tremendous importance on conversation. Their interest in the minutest details of conversation is evident from the length of time spent on exchange greetings in homes, market places, on the roadside, and in village squares. To the outsider these encounters might appear irrelevant and a waste of time and energy, but for the Igbos they form part of the emotional and social matrix uniting more serious forms of relationship. Stereotyped phrases of greeting are used to initiate conversations. Small talk is intended specifically "to break the ice of reserve as a prelude to more serious conversation."[2]

In Igboland the conventions of conversation are accorded great respect. The strategic moments are the opening and final stages of conversation. The initial stages are performed in a ritual way with "kola hospitality."[3] The regard the Igbos have for conventionalized conversation is expressly depicted by Obiechina thus:

> The expression of good-will through conventionalized conversation is so important that it has to be built into the ritual fabric of culture. Every important social or religious group-enterprise is preceded by the presentation of the kola nut, accompanied by elaborate verbal exchanges. The propriety, order, status and stability which are cultivated in traditional society are well articulated during the mock contest to establish who is the right person to break the kola nut. In such contests the art of refined conversation is at its height and is often diversified by witty sallies and light-hearted teasing, punctuated with murmurs of approbation or subdued cat-calls.[4]

The idea of conventionalizing conversation opens up the question of proverbs and folk-tales, the two most recognizable forms of Igbo oral literature.

Igbo proverbs

Proverbs, that is, brief, popular epigrams, are very commonly used by male elders as expressions of traditional wisdom and familiarity with Igbo lore. There can be no important discussion or public speech in which the elders participate that is not replete with proverbs. "Ilu bu mmanụ eji esuru okwu" [Proverb is the oil with which words are eaten], is a significant saying which expresses how the Igbos value the use of proverbs, which are a natural form of speech in all traditional societies.

Proverbs are used in settling disputes between parties, in commercial bargaining, and in all forms of oratory. It is the language of diplomacy. In the absence of written forms, the wisdom and experiences of the Igbo ancestors were preserved in proverbs. The behavior and life of the mineral, vegetable, animal and suprasensory worlds are depicted and concretized in proverbs.

Proverbs have been referred to as the kernels in which the wisdom of a traditional people is contained. In lieu of sustained philosophical exposition, proverbs serve as convenient mnemonic devices. Through them all essential events, narratives and things worth knowing are committed to memory. In this way they perform an ideological function. They make available ideas and values neatly packed in memorable and easily reproduced forms. Through use of them, the potential metaphysician finds himself immersed in a speech environment that articulates a collectively defined tradition. The latter is characterized by the existence of fixed expressions which makes up its linguistic core.

Proverbs are derived from a detailed observation of the behavior of human beings, animals, plants and nature, and in them are expressed the folklore beliefs, values, attitudes, perceptions, and emotions: indeed, the entire cultural system of Igbo society. The effectiveness as well as the force of proverbs are derived from the collective imagination that apprehends the basic principle connecting a literal fact and its allusive amplification. This collective imagination vivifies an experience by placing it beside another that has the community's seal of approval.

By making use of proverbs the individual acknowledges the primacy of the society to which he or she belongs. When I express my feeling in well-known and accepted proverbial forms, in effect I put my personal speech in a traditional context. Thus I reinforce my ideas by objectifying their validity. But in doing this I pay tribute to myself as a vehicle of traditional wisdom.

Proverbs, therefore, do not individuate the speakers. Rather, their use brings me into communion with the Igbo community. Through them I discover my being in the unity or the oneness of the community. In a way the proverbs I use mediate between my being and that of the community. "Hence my effort as a user of proverbial language is not to express my distinctiveness from the rest of the people but to indicate attachment to the community and its linguistic climate."[5]

Igbo proverbs are innumerable, broad in scope and elasticity. Examined grammatically they are the fossilized units of linguistic expression. But when they are being used to convey ideas, they prove to be very flexible and extensively manipulable. In fact, there is no experience, sensory or perceptual, that cannot find its legitimate domain of expression in proverbs. A set of proverbs can fit into a good number of different contexts. A proverb used to reflect one reality can be interpreted in another context to convey a different reality. A proverb expresses both linguistic reality and creativity. It actualizes the dreams of language and creates anew the inert mood of oral tradition. It is "an artistic device for giving complexity to narrative, unity to form, coherence and pattern to action, and direction to moral and social insights."[6] It is a mode of expressing, exploring and developing reality.

There are various strata of Igbo proverbs. Some of these are:

a. Proverbs used in the analysis of truth and sincerity, for example:

Eziokwu bụ ndu.	:	Truth is life.
Onye-mgb-oji ka onye ori nma.	:	To be a spendthrift is better than to be a rogue.

b. Proverbs depicting wisdom and foolishness, for example:

Oke mmadụ abụgh oke okwu.	:	Size does not determine the amount of wisdom or ability one has.
Adagh agwa ochinti na agha esu.	:	The effect manifests the cause.

c. Proverbs expressing the Igbo conception of life and death, for example:

Nwa nza rijuo afọ ọ·si chi ya bia were ya.	:	A prepared person does not fear death.
Ana-ene osisi kpọrọ nku anya ọdida, nke di ndu esi na ukwu bụrụ.	:	What people think will not happen may happen instead of the expected.
Chinchi gwara ụmụ ya na ife di ọkụ ga-aju oyi.	:	Patience is the key to life.

d. Proverbs on cause and effect, for example:

Ọ tibe ije agụba agadi.	:	Suitable conditions call for certain desires.
Awọ adagh agba ọsọ efifie na nkiti.	:	Nothing happens without a cause.
Ife egbe mụrụ aghagh ibu ọkụkọ.	:	People follow the pattern of their parents.

e. Proverbs expressing normality in the order of things in nature, for example:

Ibu adagh ebugide isi.	:	Things have their natural order to follow.

f. Proverbs on good and evil, for example:

Udo adagh adi ebe ajọ uche di.	:	Peace is incompatible with evil thought.
Egbe belu ugo belu, nke si ibe ya ebena, nku kwaa ya.	:	Live and let live.

g. Proverbs on time and place, for example:

Anụ naa taa, echi bụ nta.	:	Time will always be. (Shows the apparent infinity of time.)
Were ehihie chọba enwu oji maka chi ejiri.	:	Do things in their right time.

These categories of proverbs are only a select few. There are numerous others conveying moral lessons, ideas of conflict and change. Others are used in the analysis of power and personality motifs, and instill awe.

As we already noted, there are proverbs to fit into any situation in reference to both sensible and supersensible realities. But it is important to note that the use of proverbs is conventionally reserved to a certain class of people, namely, the elders and all those who by special talent or circumstance have won the approval of the ancestors to speak or officiate for the community. The community does not have to be large. It can be just a family. The oldest male of the family members, after the death of the father of the family, becomes by tradition the elder of the family. Such a person is called "Diọkpara." He can and is expected to be versed in the use of proverbs in all his public speeches. A person is by special talent approved as a member of the elder class if, due to his integrity and ability in oratory, his community chooses him as a speaker in matters relating to the public.

It is interesting to note that, apart from those who belong to the class of elders either by age, special talent or circumstance, any other person who uses proverbs must do so with caution lest he misuse them and run the risk of offending the elders and the ancestors. In the strict sense, women, children and unmarried men are not supposed to use proverbs. But they are not at all left out in the special provisions of the Igbo language. Their own specialty is folklore.

Igbo folklore

Folklore generally refers to the traditional tales or sayings preserved orally by a people. Here I am considering a noteworthy aspect of folklore in Igboland, that is, the folktales, a recognizable form of oral literature.

Folktales are characteristically anonymous: timeless and placeless tales that circulate among a people. In the traditional Igbo society they form an important channel for the informal education and entertainment of the young. The places or occasions for their narration are on the way to the farm or to streams to fetch firewood or water in the evenings, in village squares, or in common parlours (obi) after dinner. The most favourable time for the public folk-tale gathering, usually in village squares, is during moonlit nights. Such a gathering is informally supervised by one or two women, or in the absence of these, by the oldest of the children. The main function of the supervisor is to organize the little ones. From time to time she steps in during the course of the tales to correct the erring teller. The children welcome this interruption since it helps them to be sure of the correctness of their knowledge.

These folktales are usually introduced with temporal phrases, more often than not pointing to an undatable time in the past, for instance:

N'oge gboo gboo	:	In a long, long time ago . . .
N'oge gara aga	:	At a time past . . .

Sometimes if it is a story that concerns the suprasensory beings the teller begins by setting it in their land:

Na be mmuo.	:	In the abode of the suprasensory beings.
N'obodo ndi mmuo.	:	In the country of the suprasensory beings.

When the story has to do with animals, they are introduced as taking place in animal country:

Ofu mbọsi, n'ododo ụmụ anụmanụ.	:	One day, in the land of the children of animals.

No matter how and where these tales are set, they are characterized by this, namely: each is set as a happening at a vague time in the far distant past and in some undefined location. Basic to this method of setting is the establishment of the antiquity and the anonymity of the tale. These are what give each tale its worth.

One would normally expect that the anonymity of the tales would lessen their value. Paradoxically, the opposite is the case. Instead of lowering the worth or value of a tale, its anonymity highlights its universality and objectivity. It must be noted that the traditional Igbo community does not have the habit of storytelling just for mere fun or the passing of time. One purpose is, of course, to entertain the audience, usually the children. But a much more important purpose is the education of the young. This form of education brings to a focus particularly the moral fiber of the society. The folktales are laden with lessons showing that doing good yields good results whereas doing evil brings bad.

There are tales that have the purpose of teaching the proper behavior of children toward their seniors, as well as respect for parents, elders and leaders of the community. Some tales are intended to teach the techniques of becoming good housewives, of doing one's duty as parents and guardians of a family, and of knowing and carrying out one's responsibility as the leader of a kindred, clan, village or town. In a word, the cherished values of the society are instilled in the young through these folktales. This is accomplished in an indelible manner through the objectivization of the stories, an objectivization which is achieved principally by setting them in antiquity and giving them a sense of anonymity. Antiquity and anonymity have a very important meaning for the Igbos.

Still to be noted about a tale is the fact that no matter the time or place where it is set, or the characters in it, all behave like humans. Suprasensory entities, plants, trees, animate and inanimate realities can possess human attributes, for instance, appetites, virtues and vices. Animals and spirits are involved in competition like human beings. The human and non-human beings interact and communicate in a lively way. Thus the tales come across very vividly to the audience. Consequently the moral lessons or instruction which they are purported to convey come to the young in the most striking and memorable fashion.

Among the characters some are named while others are unnamed. The latter are referred to in vague terms, for example:

Ofu onye ogbenye	:	A certain poor person.
Ofu nwoke	:	A certain man.
Otu nwanyi	:	One certain woman.
Otu onye eze	:	One certain king.

The named characters usually represent particular functions in the entire body of the story, for instance:

Ogbuefi	:	Cow killer.
Nwanyi afia	:	Market woman.

Some of the names of the human figures in a tale are more definitely recognizable. In this case they usually convey a notion characteristic of the history, behavior or the peculiarities of the character in question. Animal characters are usually symbols; for instance, "Mbe," the ubiquitous tortoise, stands for a concrete embodiment of wisdom. He always avails himself of the wisdom and foolishness of his fellow animals and comes out successful in every difficult situation. A symbol of strength and power is "Agụ," the tiger. Other prominent characters are:

Atụ	:	Rhino, symbol of monstrosity.
Enyi	:	Elephant, symbol of strength, hugeness, the ultimate in any series.
Egbe	:	Hawk, a symbol of ruthlessness, agility.
Ugo	:	Eagle, symbol of beauty and excellence.
Ebili	:	Ram, symbol of gentility.

The antithesis in characterization, ideas and behaviors, is employed to emphasize certain salient lessons that the tales are supposed to convey to the audience. Comparison is also used for the same purpose. The strong, for instance, is set against the weak, the barren wife against the productive, and the wise against the foolish.

A feature of Igbo folktales is the symbolic significance of four numbers, namely: two, three, four and seven. The number two is usually used in making contrasts between opposites: big versus small, the loved one versus the hated one, the humble versus the proud. From these one can infer that the Igbos do not think philosophically in terms of an identity of opposites. They make a clear distinction between opposites in characters, ideas, behaviors, and meanings.

The number three has a very interesting symbolism. It has the idea of being the final member of a list or termination. The Igbo language has a dictum that brings this out: "Ife ruo na nke atọ ọtọ." If an event repeats itself a first time, and a second time, the third time it ceases. When three characters are represented in a story, more often than not two of the three are allied against the third.

The number four has a special significance. It is the number that designates the traditional Igbo week: Eke, Orie, Afọ, Nkwọ. Note that while three connotes a sense of the ultimate as a dead end, four is a number that is significant of propitious reality. By this I mean that the number four never designates anything adverse to man, be it a being, an event, or a character. In any situation whatsoever it occurs, the fourth in a series usually carries with it the notion of a benevolent reality.

The last of the four significant numbers in Igbo folktales is seven. It has a hazardous and unpleasant connotation. Yet many things are done in sevens. For instance, when taking the Ọzọ title (the highest public dignity title in some parts of Igboland), the candidate must have the important things to be used arranged in sevens. A suprasensory being associated with seven, carries the idea of a terrible figure of unimaginable monstrosity. When the numbers three and seven designate distance or time, there would be a long and dangerous journey to a very distant occurrence.

Another notable aspect of Igbo oral literature is its use of sobriquets. This is a metaphorical comparison of human characteristics with those of animals or plants. For example, a public speaker may refer to an opponent as Okeke, "the cat." By such an expression, the speaker manifests the traditional linguistic habit of concretizing meaning, accomplished through a direct or implied comparison with a familiar phenomenon. Thus the Igbo speaker expresses an underlying unity with nature in a manner well grasped by all.

I have introduced the topic of proverbs and folktales because they are the key to an understanding of the role of language as a channel for the metaphysics of the Igbos. The wisdom of the ancients concretized and depicted in proverbs is transmitted to the young through these tales. As fossilized expressions, proverbs are not only "the criterion of linguistic authority" in Igbo rural communities, but are over and above all the verbal expressions of the metaphysical content of Igbo thought. They are a kind of metaphysical channel insofar as they open the Igbos to an awareness of being.

In this work I do not intend to delve into tribal epics or specific panegyric poetry in order to draw out the metaphysical ingredients latent in Igbo oral literature for us to evaluate. All that is required is a thorough analysis and interpretation of everyday linguistic usage. This is so because being in its ultimate givenness is not something hidden in a remote sphere. Rather, being in the last analysis is present in its ultimate givenness to man. Its manifestation is best perceived in everydayness. Igbo oral literature in its everyday linguistic usage of fossilized expressions is able to capture the kernel of man's thought in its objectivity. In the Igbo oral tradition there is actually no dichotomy between the poetic and the prosaic, the literary and the colloquial. Metaphors, similes and figures of speech abound even in everyday, ordinary speech.

Igbo culture

Our brief consideration of the Igbo language leads us into the culture of the people since it is obvious that a language cannot be divorced from the culture which it expresses.

Culture can be seen generally as the integrated pattern of human behavior which includes thought, speech, action and artifacts transmitted to succeeding generations. Included also in elements of culture are the customary beliefs, social forms and material traits of a racial, religious or social group. Igbo culture, like all African cultures, suffered a great setback from the wheels and trails of colonialism. This is a fact that Igbo writers have lamented several times but to no avail. However, it shows how much it behooves the present generation to reconstruct our culture.

The only sure way of doing this productively is to conduct research not among the literate class of Igbo society but among Igbo "indigenes." These are those whom the present day literates refer to as "the natives." They are the elders who can neither read nor write but are the embodiment of volumes of traditional culture. They occupy a strategic position in traditional Igbo society. They are the cornerstones upholding a heavy weight, the tradition of the people. From them I gathered much during my field work. They gave me a great feeling of pride in our traditional life and culture.

"The Igbo people's close attachment to the soil and nature, the warmth of their humanity in personal relationships, their vitality and zest for life which are not circumscribed by too much planning are a cultural treasure that needs no apology."[7] Igbo culture has been handed down by word of mouth, by deeds and intimate personal contacts from antiquity to the present day through native elders. Hence, the basic concepts I will consider in my treatment of Igbo culture are tradition and community.

Community

A traditional culture cannot exist without a community. My concept of community here must be characterized as a life community, that is, a societal set-up in which there is an intimate face-to-face interaction. Relationship is on a personal, human basis as distinguished from the predominantly impersonal relationship that exists in today's urban societies, where everyone minds his or her own business and frequently does not even know the next-door neighbor.

In an Igbo community which embodies traditional culture, there is cooperation among people residing permanently in a single locality. The members of such a community share the basic conditions of a common life. The physical proximity, the enduring character of their social relationships, the relative similarity of activities and status of its members constitute the peculiarities of such a community. The community strives to maintain the different groups within it while maintaining itself as a community. Hence the life and purpose of the community come, in certain matters, before the individual interests of the members.

The community life begins in the family. The marriage bond ties together the young couple from whom the future members of the family must come. The Igbos maintain a very strong family system. A family is not formed until all the marriage customs are fulfilled. When a young man and a young lady encounter each other, they do not rush off to court and rattle off promises before a judge, without a moment's thought of their implications. A long and protracted series of customary ceremonies must be performed to prepare for the important task of marriage. It is not a matter that concerns only the young man and lady. The process of getting married involves families, relatives, and sometimes even the clans and villages of each party. This undertaking can not be hurried because the people are aware of the fact that marriage is a lifelong undertaking.

In a traditional Igbo society, a young man does not choose a young lady for marriage because she is beautiful or very attractive. In fact, a girl of extraordinary attractiveness runs the risk of not getting a marriage partner all her life. A lady does not choose to marry a man because he is handsome or a great lover. Marriages based on these reasons are not regarded as marriages at all.

The principle that dictates the choice of a marriage partner is based on the Igbo notion of life and existence. The Igbos have a very high regard for life. Life is not a personal business which can be tampered with at will. Life and existence are not properties that belong wholly and entirely to individuals. They belong also to the community of being formed by dead ancestors, the living, and over and above all, they belong to Chineke, the author and sustainer of life and existence. In choosing a marriage partner, therefore, a man is aware of the fact that he is taking a decision to bring new life and new existence into the family, into his community of being. He is about to let the ancestors adopt this new life and existence. Hence, the man's decision must be made with caution. The will of his family, the elders, the ancestors, and above all that of Chineke must be taken into consideration.

In the same manner does the girl go about arriving at a decision.

Hence full scale inquiries are conducted by each party. The man's party leaves no stone unturned in inquiring into the history and genealogy of the girl's family, and *vice versa*. The aim of each party's investigation is to find out two things: a. Is the young man or the lady of good character? What family background has he or she? Has the family a history of fertility or sterility? b. Is the lady's community of being willing to hand the lady over to become forever one with the man's community of being?

It is only when these preliminaries are taken care of that official steps towards performing the customary stipulations are undertaken. The first of these is the official breaking of the ice, that is, the mutual exchange of the wish of the man and the lady: "I would like to marry you." This is done in the presence of the parents of the lady and the family representatives of the man. After this, other ceremonies are performed within a period of time. Until all is accomplished, the man and the lady cannot live together.

It is not within the scope of this study to go deeper into the interesting details of these marriage ceremonies. Suffice it to say here that the Igbo community has a strong family system as a pivot on which it revolves, and this system is based on Igbo metaphysical conceptions of life and existence.

It is important to mention here the father–son relationship. This relationship is crucial to the traditional system. It is the basis of ancestral authority upon which the continuity of the institutions, values, attitudes and sentiments of Igbo culture depends. It has its root in the Igbo theory of duality, according to which whatever is happening in this world has its replica in the suprasensory world. A man knows fully that the way he treats his son is the way his own father now existing in the suprasensory world must treat him and his family. The son strives to be reverent and obedient to his father because he knows that respect to his father means respect to the ancestors and to Chineke. It means being identified with the totality of all that is.

Other things could be discussed in connection with Igbo family and community systems, for example: the network of rights and obligations that accompany the Igbo family setup, the matrix of economic, political and religious relations involved in the community system. All these are important but I do not consider them to be of immediate relevance to the present work.

Accompanying the concept of community in Igbo culture is the notion of tradition. Community is structured the way it is on account of Igbo adherence to the stipulations of tradition.

Tradition

Tradition by definition can mean an inherited pattern of thought or action, such as a religious practice or a social custom. It also means cultural continuity in social attitudes and institutions. The Igbo concept of tradition includes all these and more. The Igbo word for tradition is "omenani." It is also translated as "obibendi," that is, "according to what is accepted in one's community."

"Omenani" comes from two roots, ome and ani. Ome denotes action, dynamic activity. It has the same root as "omume," which means action, act, conduct, doing. This in turn has the same root as "omimi," which means mystery, depth.

"Ani" means land, ground, soil. It is also the name used for the earth-god, the highest and most universal god in Igboland. She is regarded as the "foster mother" of all men. On her lap man is born and there he spends his whole life.[8] Ani is the terrestial expression of Chineke, the all-embracing supra-sensory being.

To get a comprehensive idea of the Igbo concept of "omenani" we have to join to the usual dictionary meaning of "tradition" the notions of ome, omume, omimi on the one hand, and the notion of ani on the other. Drawing upon my discussions with Igbo elders, I would think of omenani as an inherited pattern of thought and action customarily and mysteriously in harmony with the dynamic creativity of being within the totality of all that is.

The essential requirement of omenani (tradition) on the part of the individual is the identification of the individual with the totality of being. This identification is manifested in the individual's compliance with the specific beliefs and customs prevalent in the community. Values based exclusively on individual self-interest, as is prevalent in modern urban society, are out of place here. The interest of the community of being supercedes that of the individual.

It is important to note that this concept of omenani does not say or mean that the socio-political ordering among the Igbos is communist. As E. Obiechina remarked:

> It would be wrong to interpret the concentration on common goals and the primacy of the common interest as a matter of suppression of the personality from the outside, of constraint on the part of an authority. Social conformity and the discouragement of deviation from the common norms of behavior are not the same thing as the repressive curbing of individual freedom. Social freedom is in the final analysis related to legality and this is commonly expressed as the principle of the greatest good of the greatest number. Tradi-

tional social philosophy is based on this principle and because it is fundamental to the very survival and general health of the society, is given validity by being anchored in customary practice and protected by divine and ancestral authority.[9]

The members of a village community are traditionally united by the bonds of a common belonging. Every member is fully welcome and recognized. Rights and obligations are defined within the community structure. They are inviolable because they bear the stamp of custom and omenani and are sanctioned by the authority of the ancestors. Taboos and prohibitions are not seen as repressive laws. They are part of the normal routine of life that saves the community from the unwarranted intervention of individuals and assures the freedom of each and every member of the community.

Any breach in the unity of omenani is regarded as a breach of peace likely to result in some tragedy for the individual as well as for the community. Hence this breach is treated as a community affair. For instance, if a man commits a crime, be it theft or murder, the Igbos do not wait for the police to come to start mulling over the matter under the pretense of conducting a high-powered investigation. The Igbo traditional response is that the first people to catch a glance of the culprit instantaneously pounce on him or her and exert the appropriate justice once and for all. If it is an offense that deserves death, willful murder, for instance, the people will kill the murderer on the spot and finish with the case then and there.

This instantaneous action of the community is based on the principle that delaying justice is breaking the omenani whose fundamental *raison d'être* is ensuring peace and harmony in the community of being. The man who has willfully removed another's life has *de facto* and *de iure* lost the right to his own life. He is a danger to the community. But because no individual has the right to remove another's life (not even that of the murderer), it is the community which has the full right to deprive the criminal of his life. Hence the people on the spot automatically rally around and administer justice. Thus peace and harmony are restored without undue delay. People of violence are forever kept out of the society. In fact, traditional Igbos find the institution of agencies of force like the police an impediment to justice and peace. A would-be criminal who knows that if he is caught committing a crime, the police will protect him from immediate justice—at worst they put him in prison where he has still a chance of escaping one day—has really nothing to stop him from going ahead and committing crimes. The Igbo mentality is that where the police operate, more crimes and disorder abound.

In time of difficulty the whole community reacts as a unit to exact redress if even one member is offended by another community. The community also comes out to make amends even if only one member of their group offends another community. In cases requiring peaceful settlements, the method is conciliatory rather than contractual or rigidly legalistic. Presiding over such cases are the elders, the community spokesmen, and over and above all, the ancestors. The final verdict is to be pronounced by the ancestors through Onye Nze (the holder of ọfọ, the symbol of justice and ancestral authority).

The spirit of omenani is always linked with the sense of mystery and the supernatural. The idea of making sure that all is in tune with the community of being which includes the sensory and the suprasensory realities is always in the background of the thought and actions of the people, whether they are thinking and acting as a community or as individuals.

The Igbo socio-religious milieu

In a work on African cultural history, Basil Davidson observed that the Igbos:

> uncommonly among Africans have been markedly success oriented, egalitarian but individualistic; they have thought it an essential aspect of the 'right and natural' that talent should lead to enterprise, and enterprise to promotion, and promotion to privilege. They have insistently stressed social mobility.[10]

My research and experience confirm this observation. Moreover, it is important to note from the outset the close relation between Igbo social and religious life. In Igbo communities social and religious units are hardly distinguishable. The social setup is also closely connected with political organization. Consequently a quest of the socio-religious mentality of the people implies a political dimension.

The traditional governmental instuments are the family leaders, age-grade associations, title-making societies, and dibia[11] fraternities. The stages of socio-religious groupings discernible are: the family structure, the ụmụnna unit, the village unit and the town unit.

The nuclear family (Ezina-ụnọ) comprises a man, his wife and their children as well as their dependents. The man as the head of the family represents all the members individually and collectively as occasions demand in relation to other social units. Officiating as their spiritual leader, he pours out libations on their behalf and blesses them. The "ọfọ-staff" which he holds symbolises his political and religious authority. Thus he combines the office of political leadership and priesthood.

The Obi (Umunna)

The next stage in the Igbo social group structure is the Obi, that is, the extended family structure. When the male descendants of the nuclear family grow to maturity and marry, they, their wives and children still have a social connection as belonging to one large family. They are the extended family members. In some places, this structure comes under such names as ụmụ-eke, ụmụ-n'onovo, that is, children of the mother of onovo, etc. In this case the head of the entire household is called the ọkpara, the eldest living male descendant of the eldest son of the nuclear family. Again, like the head of the family, he performs social, political and religious functions on behalf of the extended family. Everybody looks up to him for leadership, counseling, and blessing. He settles problems regarding marriages, land and similar minor matters. It is also part of his function to officiate in naming ceremonies by conferring names on the newly-born babies of the family. He enjoys much respect and honor because of his age and more because of his office. As circumstances demand, he may summon the ụmụnna to handle in a democratic fashion matters that are beyond his arbitration.

The Ọfọ

The greatest treasure that the ọkpara of the family guards is the ọfọ of the family. This is a small piece of wood taken from a special type of tree called osisi-ọfọ (the tree of ọfọ). This piece of wood is usually smeared with blood and ornamented with strips of light feather around the edge of one of the ends. As "symbolic of power and authority and employed as a law and order enforcement agency, it is a type of staff of judgment that the Ọkpara holds when arbitrating disputes in the ụmụnna circle."[12]

The ọfọ is also used in ritual celebrations. John Boston noted that "the Igbo believes that no ritual of any kind is valid unless an ọfọ is used."[13] Also W. G. R. Horton, referring to the Ibagwa Igbo in Nsukka, observed that the ọfọ is a sort of official stamp which validates the existence of cult, social groups and individuals with whom it is associated, by linking them to Chukwu, the ultimate source of all life."[14]

The ideas expressed by both Boston and Horton are, to be sure, correct. Yet I see a greater and deeper metaphysical significance in the ọfọ. It brings out clearly the Igbo notion of being as a totality, as a unity. Between the visible sphere and the realm of the unseen there is continuous communication and interaction. Among the living there is much concern whether the totality of the community of being is acting as one. The ọkpara uses the ọfọ to secure this assurance. When he holds the ọfọ-staff, he is assured that he is no longer alone in his decisions, judgment and benedictions. The entire community of being, embracing the living and the ancestors, is solidly behind him. He is beyond his individuality.

By holding the ọfọ-staff in his hand when dealing with matters relating to the extended family, he is aligning himself with the visible as well as the unseen members of the family, the ancestors. Hence the ọfọ is used to maintain and perpetuate the spirit of tradition, the purpose of which is the assurance of the continuity of the community.

The Kindred

A group of localized, patrilineal members make up a kindred. They can be called ụmụnna (children of the same father), but may not be referred to as ụmụnne (children of the same mother). This is so because all the members of a kindred may be able to trace their lineage back to one father but not necessarily to one mother. In this unit the oldest living male descendant of the eldest son of the original founder of the kindred holds the ọfọ and performs the functions of the ọkpara with accompanying rights and obligations.

The Village-unit (Ogbe)

This comes next to the kindred in extension and comprises various localized, patrilineal, socio-religious units that in a very remote past could trace their origin back to a common founder. The village has its senior branch, the subdivision which represents the descendants of the eldest man in this branch holds the village ọfọ with the title of ọkpara.

It is pertinent to know that succession to the office of ọkpara, be it in obi, ụmụnna or village, is according to the adelphic principle. Thus it passes not from father to son but rather from the incumbent to his next brother in line.

Government at the village level follows the pattern of direct democracy involving all lineages within a circumscribed area. All the male adults participate in the social and political organizations of the members with due respect and deference usually made to the ọkpara as the traditional head of the ogbe.

The Town unit (Obodo)

This is the largest socio-religious grouping in Igboland. It comprises several village units. Obiego[15] describes this as a socio-religious grouping founded on a number of principles: firstly, it is a local unit in that its inhabitants occupy a common territory. Secondly, it is a mythical kinship unit. Many towns have legendary accounts to substantiate how their units originated, or how their founders came into being and begot children. Thus members of the same town often have some tradition of a common origin or of some kind of common descent.

Unlike the village unit, an obodo usually has a communally accepted guardian or patron who is supposed to be the invisible symbol of solidarity in the whole town. The name of the guardian varies according to what aspect of nature is emphasized in the town. For instance, in Okija it is Ulasi, the name of the biggest river in the town; in Obosi it is Idemili (an area of marsh), while at Akpugo it is Ani-Akpugo (mother earth of Akpugo). The chief priest of the town is the visible symbol of the patron.

Prior to 1977 only a few towns in Igboland had recognized political heads. These few included Onitsha (the Obi of Onitsha), and Aguata (the Obi of Aguata). Since 1978, with the establishment by the Nigerian government of the House of Chiefs, there has been a proliferation of political leaders. This proliferation has been so extensive that in some states a town has several autonomous chiefs. For example, Akpugo in the Nkanu local government area, a town that had no unanimously recognized chiefs prior to 1977, now enjoys the hegemony of five autonomous chiefs, each influential in his own portion of the town.

It is noteworthy that even with the chiefdoms instituted in Igbo towns, the governmental system is still democratic. The Okparas in different villages still perform their social, political and religious duties. The chief (where there is only one in the town) shares with the chief priest of the town's patron the social, political and religious functions with their accruing rights and obligations.

The chief priests play a vital role in the community. They normally officiate at public religious ceremonies as well as at certain social and political functions. To the Igbos they occupy the highest place in the hierarchy of sensible reality. This is necessitated by the nature of their function of being a link between the sensory and the suprasensory world.

Having completed our preliminary discussion of Igbo language, culture, and socio-religious structure, we are now better prepared to understand the second and the main part of this study. Needless to say, our treatment of these cultural items has not been exhaustive. However, I think it sufficient to lead us into Igbo metaphysics proper.

Review Questions

1. Identify and explain the two main avenues to the thought-content of any people.

2. Underline the importance of oral tradition in this study.

3. Explain briefly why the consideration of culture as the integrated pattern of human behavior is necessary for an understanding of the philosophy of the Igbos.

4. Show how community and tradition are the basic concepts in the Igbo culture. Explain in detail the Igbo understanding of "omenani."

5. "A quest of the socio-religious mentality of the people implies a political dimension." Briefly state your arguments either in defense or against this view.

Part Two

Toward a description of metaphysics

Normally the term physics refers to the study of nature in general, and metaphysics comes after it. The questions relating to metaphysics arise out of, but go beyond, factual or scientific questions about the world. Traditionally metaphysics in the broad sense would include cosmology, ontology and theodicy. Cosmology discusses the origin, structure and space-time relations of the universe. Ontology asks what is the "reality" of propositions and numbers? Is existence a predicate or a property? Theodicy relates to the philosophy of religion in questions such as: Does anything exist necessarily? Why is there something rather than nothing?

A distinctive feature of metaphysics is the universality of its questions. In as much as it seeks an inventory of the kinds of things that exist, it also asks what can be said about anything that exists insofar as it exists. Are all beings that exist classifiable into different fundamental types, that is, categories? Can there be any hierarchy of kinds of entities? Are some dependent on others for their existence? Questions involving the relations between very general notions such as thing, entity, object, individual, universal, particular, substance, event, process, state, etc., likewise constitute a special field of metaphysical investigation.

If we examine the genesis of metaphysics, we notice that there are several general characteristics that can be distinguished. However, for our purposes here, with some simplification, we distinguish three major outlooks. Our characterization of three groups does not mean that they do not overlap: surely they differ but they are not totally distinguished.

First, the Platonic outlook: this takes one or more substances as the basis of the universe. It is connected with attitudes towards change. The fact of change led Plato to investigate enduring reality and our knowledge of it. Others, Parmenides, Spinoza, and those we call monists, maintained either that change is not fully real or that the most basic things do not change except in secondary or unimportant ways.

Second, the Aristotelian view was formulated to understand change and postulated potency and act as the substantive basis of all that is. From Aristotle are derived those distinctions that have played an important role in the history of thought such as essence and existence, matter and form, and substance and accident.

Third, the Heraclitian outlook depicts events and processes as the basis of the universe. The stoics, Hegel, Bergson, and Whitehead can be located within this camp. For them change is at the heart of all things. "Change," Nietzsche remarked, "is an eternal recurrence of the same cycle; and endless repetition of exactly the same world history." In this perspective, unity and constancy are accepted as real but dependent essentially on change.

An examination of the nature and kinds of change reveals the import of the distinctions between potency, act, privation, matter and form. These distinctions, in turn, lead to the question of matter and substance and their relations to space and time. The discussion of space and time opens up a whole dimension of problems regarding their reality, nature, absoluteness, and uniqueness.

The discussion of space and time in metaphysics inevitably involves one in the question of infinity. Is the universe finite or infinite? Did it have a beginning in time or was it eternal? Through the centuries these questions have agitated religious thinkers. The history of Western metaphysics echoes the debates on these topics of Neoplatonists, early and medieval Christians, Muslims, and Jews.

From this brief sketch of the areas covered by Western metaphysics, one thing is clear: namely, that metaphysics is a search for an understanding of beings in their ultimate causes. It seeks a description and identification of the intelligible nature, structure and characteristic qualities of reality. As a search for meaning, metaphysics is an inquiry into the intelligibility and the value of reality. Bearing in mind this description of metaphysics together with the areas it covers, let us now approach Igbo metaphysics with an Igbo mind, freed as far as possible from the presuppositions and controversies of Western philosophical thought.

chapter three

The Origin, structure, and purpose of the universe

The Origin

The question of the origin of the visible world does not seem to pose a serious problem for the Igbos. They have a proverb that goes like this: "Ife welu mbido g'enwe njedebe" (Whatever has a beginning will have an end.) They watch things come and go. A child is born, matures, and after living at most a hundred and some years, passes away. The animal kingdom is ruled by the same cycle. Seeds also germinate, grow to maturity, and later wither away. From the observance of the process of the coming-to-be and ceasing-to-be of visible reality, one draws the obvious inference: whatever has a beginning has an end. Therefore, the visible world has a beginning. Thus the Igbo thinker reasons to the possibility of a beginning for all visible entities.

Some Igbo folk-tales are usually introduced and set in a peculiar manner to bring out the fact of a beginning of beginnings: "N'oge gboo, oge ụwa n'adirọ ọbụ sọ ndi muọ di" (In a long, long time ago when the visible world was not, only the unseen were.) Here the folk story teller begins his tale by introducing and setting it at an undatable moment. "N'oge gboo gboo," a familiar expression used to refer to the very distant past when there was nothing in existence, indicates the 'before,' the time prior to the beginning of beginnings.

Note that in Igbo thought even at the moment before visible beginnings the unseen realities were in existence: Ọbụ sọ ndi muọ di (only the unseen beings were.) What, then, is the relationship between the unseen beings and the fact of the origin of visible realities? A sample Igbo account of the origin of the visible things can depict for us the people's mentality.

This is an account of the origin of fire. In a long, long time ago a group of animals set out on a very distant journey to the land of the unseen. They were to cross seven deep rivers and seven lands. Antelope, the fastest of them, ran past all but could not cross even the first river. Elephant, the heaviest of them, got stuck in the mud of one of the rivers. Some animals could wade across some of the rivers but were stuck in the sixth or seventh. Finally, only the dog and the frog crossed all the rivers. On reaching the end of their journey, each of them was given, by the head of the inhabitants of the land of the unseen beings, a gift of fire to bring over to the world of the visible. Both messengers accepted this gift and made their way back home. On their way home the dog proudly said to the frog: "I will run faster than you and bring fire to the world and I will be the one known for bringing such a gift to mankind." The frog said humbly: "Well, I will move only at my own pace."

They continued their journey. Soon the dog outpaced the frog and crossed all the seven rivers. By this time it became very hungry. As it was nearing home it perceived the scent of dog food. It was attracted and diverted into the bush to find the food. When it saw the food, it immediately dropped the fire which it had gripped with its mouth and began to eat the food. At the end it turned to pick up the fire but discovered that it was nowhere to be seen. Then it remembered that the head of the inhabitants of the land of the unseen had warned them not to drop the fire until they reached home. Meanwhile, the frog had crossed all the rivers, passed where the dog was eating and did not even perceive the smell of any food. Eventually it was the frog that successfully brought fire to mankind. But by the time it reached the visible world the fire had so illumined the bearer that the frog and fire had become one. The frog had turned into fire.

This is typical of Igbo folktales that are intended to teach origins. Every useful object on the earth has a tale describing its origin. Origins are always traced back to the land of the unseen. Hence, visible objects are to be understood as gifts from the head of the inhabitants of the unseen.

As this is a folktale, there is no question of providing a factual demonstration of the story; its incongruities are of no concern. All we are concerned with here is what it demonstrates: that even though the Igbos see material realities come to be and cease to be, they know that there is an unseen which serves as the basis of the movements of coming-to-be and ceasing-to-be. Thus we see the relationship between the unseen beings and the fact of the origin of the visible realities: the visible realities have their origin in the unseen beings, the inhabitants of the invisible world.

Existence of two worlds

From the above sample Igbo account of the origin of the visible things it is clear that the Igbos recognize the existence of two worlds: the visible and the invisible. *Uwa* (world) is the Igbo term for the visible world. The term used for the invisible world is *Ani Muo* (land of the unseen). If we are looking for an Igbo term that is equivalent to the English idea of *universe*, that is, the totality of what is, we have to combine the two terms *uwa* and *ani muo*. This would give us something like *Uwa N'ani muo*. The modern Igbo ways of characterizing the "universe" are *uwaa n'uwa ozo* (this world and another world) and *enu igwe n'uwa* (the top of the sky and the earth).

If you ask an Igbo elder the question: How do you know that there are two worlds?, his answer will be unhesitatingly: "It is evident." By this he means that the fact that two worlds exist is implied in the people's way of life. It is made practical in different religious observances. For example, a traditional Igbo begins his day by calling together all the members of his household to *igo ofo*[1] (morning prayer). The ceremony begins with the officiant's washing of his hands and face and entering his "Obi," the parlour where the whole family usually gathers. Sitting in the middle of the room, he takes a cup of palm wine (at times a piece of kola nut may be used in place of wine). He sips the wine and then spits it out on the floor. When he has repeated this, he then recites the following invocations:

Ndi bi' n'enu :	Those living up
nwuru mmaya . . .	drink wine . . .
Ndi bi n'ani :	Those living below
nwuru mmaya . . .	drink wine . . .
Okike kelu ife :	Creator who created
nalu mmaya .	beings take wine
nwuo . . .	and drink.

He then pours wine on the ground each time he invokes any of the invisible entities.

This brief description of the igo ofo ceremony prompts certain observations. Both the actions and the words of the traditional Igbo indicate that there is communication between the people of the visible world and entities of an invisible sphere. The act of splashing the wine on the floor attests the people's firm belief that there are present among them invisible beings ready to share with them from a common source. The tone of the prayers addressed to the invisible entities is a further witness to this belief: the conviction of the existence of an invisible world whose inhabitants can influence the going and comings of beings in the visible world.

When I asked my informant further on this point: "Are you really sure that there are two worlds?," his reply was couched in the following proverb: "Ada agwa ochinti n'agha di" (One does not tell the deaf that a battle is on.) This proverb goes to the core of the matter. For just as even a deaf person need not wait to be informed that a battle has begun because he sees it, so we do not question the existence of two world because the activities of everyday life imply it.

Man is caught up within the boundaries of these two worlds. "Uwa" (the visible world) is evident since it is experienced by the senses, especially those of sight and touch. "Ani muọ" (the invisible world) is to the Igbo a reality because it is an accepted fact of everyday activity.

The question is: Why is the existence of the invisible world an accepted fact to the Igbos? In other words, why do they make the distinction between the visible and the invisible worlds and hold onto the reality of these two worlds?

There is reason to think that the distinction is grounded in religion because most religions take for granted the existence of another world, the world to which we belong after death. As I have indicated,[2] Igbos are deeply religious, and their religious sentiments and beliefs can hardly be divorced from their everyday activities. Hence their acceptance of the existence of the invisible world as a fact could stem from their religious belief in life after death.

However, I would like to examine the Igbo distinction between two worlds from two standpoints: first, the idea of reincarnation; second, the Igbo concept of death.

The idea of reincarnation: E. G. Parrinder and many other writers on African peoples have observed: "Reincarnation to most Africans, is a good thing. It is a return to this sunlit world for a further period of invigorating life."[3]

The Igbos are among this group of Africans. Their idea that human beings can come back to life after death is basic to their conception of reality. The argument is this: if human beings after passing away from this visible world can come back after a certain period has elapsed and be born again, there must have been a place where they remained within that period. That place could not have been this visible world; otherwise they would still be continuously visible to the living and not have passed away. It must be a place completely different from this material world in terms of imperceptibility to the senses and, as such, must be an entirely different world of its own, a world where the human beings who have left this material world remain until they are able to be reincarnated. Hence there must be two worlds in existence, the visible world and the world unseen, that is, ani muọ.

The Igbo concept of death: Critics might say that the validity of the above argument depends on whether or not reincarnation[4] is a reality. This is true. Hence an alternative argument that makes use of the Igbo concept of death may be necessary. Even though the Igbos mourn their dead with grief and extend sympathy, as do other people, they are well aware that death is not an end but a transition. If a person dies, he is born into another life completely different from the one he had. This is the case with the ancestors. This new life cannot be without a place in which it is being lived. There must, therefore, be a world other than this visible world where the ancestors are dwelling and from where they exercise some influence on the goings and comings of the living. Thus the Igbos arrive at the fact that there must be two worlds.

For a Western reader to grasp how the Igbos have come to make this distinction, it is necessary to consider what Innocent I. Egbujie described as "the occult phenomena which are daily experiences in African culture."[5] An occult phenomenon whether of the good or of the evil type is an event that takes place at a special rendezvous which, according to the belief of the people, is an intermediate place between the invisible world and the visible world. Here the spirits or the spiritual parts of men hold meetings with the nonhuman spirits. Naturally, an outsider wants to know what the belief is that is operative behind this outlook. How did Africans originally experience the world so as to arrive at such a belief?

> For the Africans the world is *dual in nature.* Beyond and over above the visible, tactile, physical world, there is a non-visible, nontactile world which envelopes the former. It permeates the former through and through; it is simultaneously within and outside of the earth and the seas.[6]

For the Igbos, that enveloping world is the abode of nonhuman spirits, both good and bad. Some of the good spirits or gods are the earth, sun, sea, sky and wind gods, as well as the gods of the chief crops and the ancestral gods comprised of the spirits of dead ancestors—the men and women who lived good and virtuous lives on earth. The bad spirits are those of men and women who lived evil and abominable lives on earth. The common belief is that these spirits have secret societies: the good spirits participate in good and well-meaning societies, and the bad spirits engage in evil societies. However, the bad spirits are circumscribed by our enveloping cosmos, whereas the good spirits reach the abode of the King God (Chukwu) and come back to the intermediate world they inhabit so as to be near to the living in order to protect, guide and benefit them. Among these good spirits is the invisible self of each human person, a good spirit more or less similar, it has been argued, to the Christian guardian angel.

The answer to the question how the Igbos arrive at the notion of, and belief in, a spiritual world enveloping the visible one can be understood thus. Among the Igbos, as with every other people, fortune and misfortune are commonplaces of daily experience. There is an Igbo saying that if you see something dancing on top of the sea, you must know there is another something underneath the waters playing the tune. So it is with fortune and misfortune. Their causes are not too far removed from the physical world of men. The good spirits, or gods, as the ambassadors of God are harbingers of good fortune. The bad spirits are the 'tune-players' of misfortune.

In brief, the Igbo concept is that for a man to be truly human and successful in life, he must be in constant relationship with the good spirits. These gods have power over evil spirits who, in turn, try to avoid confrontation with the good spirits. One thing to be noted is that the good spirits respect the freedom of man. Thus, if a man repeatedly opts to do evil. the good spirits automatically withdraw their protective power. The man then falls victim to the evil spirits who take hold of him and confirm him in evil ways. He eventually dies a bad man to join the company of the evil spirits in their invisible domain.

Normally the Igbos dread these evil spirits, but everyone knows that he can overcome them by observing the laws of the land as prescribed by the Earth-god. Amos Tutuola has written in his novel, *My Life in the Bush of Ghosts*, a forceful account of this invisible world of spirits. He gives an account of his life in the 'Bush' of ghosts where he fell in among evil spirits.[7] Also, Chinua Achebe, in *Things*

Fall Apart, has referred to the Egwugwu whose quavering voice
". . . filled the air as these spirits of the ancestors, just emerged from
the earth, greeted themselves in their esoteric language."[8] Achebe is
talking of the good spirits who have emerged from the earth because
their invisible habitat permeates the physical earth through and
through.

From what we have seen so far, one may conclude that for the
Igbos there is a functional unity of the physical, utilitarian world
with the deified, unchanging world that has shed its materiality.
This is the environment in which the Igbo people, like all other
African peoples, are born, live, and die. Immersed in this environment, the people naturally develop the conviction of the existence
of two worlds. Because they are much more inclined to be practical
than speculative, they tend to make the two worlds equally real, as
if both were material. Thus they express the spiritual concepts connected with the invisible world in a material mode.

The Igbo theory of duality

The Igbo idea of the existence of two worlds can be further
understood in terms of what the writings of some indigenous Igbo
scholars imply, namely; an Igbo theory of duality[9] which says that
for all beings in the material universe, existence is a dual and inter-
related phenomenon. Whatever exists in a sensible form in this
world does not exist solely in this way. It has a dual existence, dual
in the sense that the reality of its existence is a phenomenon in the
visible world and also a reality in the invisible world. Whatever ob-
tains here has its replica in the world of the unseen.

To exemplify what I call the Igbo theory of duality, let us recall
what was said in chapter two concerning Igbo ways of choosing a
marriage partner. The principle underlying the Igbo method of making this choice is based on the notion of life and existence. In making a decision to marry, a young man knows that he is taking a normally irrevocable step to bring a new life into the family, a new
existence into his community of being.

Within this community of being are the two main divisions in
the Igbo concept of the universe tht we have mentioned. Uwa (the
world of the visible) and ani muọ (the world of the unseen). And so,
life, the existence that is added through marriage to the family of a
man, becomes a phenomenon, an event taking place in the visible
world because it involves visible and sensible entities. But it does
not end there. Whatever happens here occurs likewise in the sphere

of the unseen. The twofold community of being of the woman is handed over to a new community of being in both the visible and invisible realms. Because, therefore, this transfer of life and existence is effected on two levels, the wills of both the visibles and the invisibles are meticulously sought before marriage is contracted.

This theory of duality is not restricted to human beings. It is also applicable to all material things. This can be deduced from the Igbo cultural way of handling material things. Take the farmer's way of handling his yams.[10] When he gathers his yams into his barn, he handles them with care. If it happens that in the process of lifting a tuber of the yams, it falls and breaks on the ground, he immediately picks up the broken pieces whispering thus: "Eze ji amarọ m ụma kwuli gi,"—(King of yams, I did not willfully break you).

To an outsider it may appear either that the farmer is talking to the materially visible broken pieces of yam, or that the dictum is the farmer's defense of himself. But neither of these is correct. The farmer is showing his respect for the invisible element contained in the visible. This invisible element is regarded by the farmer as having its existence in the land of the unseen. If the dictum were the farmer's defense of himself, it would be used only to show some remorse of conscience when an injury is done to a human being. But among the Igbos such a dictum is very commonly used when any material object in daily use is misused or in some way mishandled. This type of dictum is also used by the dibia (traditional Igbo priest) when he is praying over stones, ornamented pieces of wood (ọfọ) and other utensils which make up his objects of worship. As he speaks or whispers to them directly, he knows that he is communicating, not with the visible objects as such, but with the invisible element contained in them.

In the mind of the Igbos the invisible element in any material object is equally as real as the visible aspect of the same object. If we judge from the degree of attention paid to the visible element, it would not be wrong to conclude that the unseen element is much more esteemed than the visible.

In the traditional Igbo community, before a man slaughters an animal for food, a goat, for instance, he normally murmurs the following words: "Oke amadi kam yọtagi anyinyọọ." "Oke amadi" is a respectful way of referring to the invisible element of the goat. Literally, the whole expression means: "Invisible part of the goat, let me obtain a favor from you." In other words, the man seeks the permission of the invisible element before he kills the visible part of the animal.

Because they consider both the visible and the invisible aspects of a thing as real, the Igbos usually tend to give some degree of respect to material objects, especially those in daily use.

Significantly, for the Igbo the invisible nature as well as the visible are metaphysically real, a fact evidenced in their language. In personal conversations as well as communal discussions, references are commonly made to "Ife na ife ya na ya yi" (that is, a thing and that with which it is.) A careful analysis of the expression "ife ya na ya yi" will reveal an interesting insight. The English expression "that with which it is" does not actually bring out the exact meaning of the Igbo sense. In the Igbo language "ife ya na ya yi" can mean two things. First, it can mean something which is entirely distinct from the visible part of an object. In this sense it strongly implies that the unseen part of a material object is metaphysically real and distinct from the visible. This would in fact show that for the Igbos there is sharp duality of visible and invisible parts of a material object.

But the Igbo expression 'ife ya na ya yi" can also be used in an Aristotelian sense of "that by which something is." This would show that the Igbo expression "ife ya na ya yi" indicates that for the Igbos there is some element of the unseen part of a material object in the visible. In other words, the invisible element is distinct from and yet part of the visible, and in fact it is "that by which the visible is." This second interpretation of the Igbo expression "ife ya na ya yi" helps us to understand why the Igbos seem to esteem the unseen element much more than the visible. It also helps us to comprehend why, in the case of the broken yam, the farmer could address the unseen through the visible: the visible, sensible element, exists only in combination with the unseen; and whereas the two are distinct from each other, the latter is that by which the former is. From this we can say that the Igbos both maintain a sharp duality, and conceive of the unseen element as being that by which the visible element is. Thus it seems that the duality is moderated.

Since the visible, sensible element, "Ife ewelu ike imetu aka," (that which can be touched) exists only in combination with the invisible, the latter cannot be construed as existing without the former. A lump of matter, for example, is identified as such because of that by which it is traditionally known to be what it is. If an Igbo elder is confronted with a material object, he examines it and identifies it as a yam only if it shows signs of having the essential properties traditionally known to be associated with yams.

From the last point, it seems evident that the Igbos are using the theory of duality to handle what in the Western philosophy is known as the problem of the universals. In the case of the Igbo elder examining a yam, is he not making the move from the particular to the universal? He is looking for the features that the material object before him shares in common with other objects of the same genus. Put differently, he is actually determining whether the object before him could be an instance of the general notion of yam. Implicit philosopher that he is, he is involved in essential determination or definition. So without mentioning it explicitly, the Igbos in their own way are dealing with the problem of universals. Even though it is not yet developed, one cannot doubt that it is there, even if it is only in embryo. Any attempt to discuss this problem here will involve the use of Western categories. Hence we have treated it in the appendix rather that in the main body of this work.[11]

The theory of duality
and the soul-body unity in man

A reflection on the Igbo idea of the existence of two worlds and its deeper understanding in the theory of duality reveals that the distinctions thus made are leading up to the Igbo way of grappling with the age-old philosophical problem of the soul–body unity in man. A clarification of Igbo terminology is important here because it will help to determine the nature of this unity.

The Igbo word for body is *aru*, also called *ahu* in some parts of Igboland. *Ahu* has a common root with *ihu* which means to see with the eyes. Thus *ahu* or *aru* has the notion of being visible, that is, perceptible by the senses.

The Igbos are not unanimous regarding the original terminology for the soul. Three hypotheses can be examined, namely:

    a. Mkpulu-obi
    b. Chi;
    c. Muo.

Mkpulu-obi hypothesis: The exponents of this hypothesis think that the correct term for soul in the Igbo language is "mkpulu-obi" which literally means the nut or seed of the heart. The main argument in favor of this hypothesis is that it emphasizes the importance of the soul. I hesitate to accept this for the following reasons. First, the term mkpulu-obi was not originally widely used in the Igbo language. It came into prominence with the advent of the missionaries in an effort by the catechists to interpret the preachers' idea of the English word, *soul*. Second, the term conveys the idea of the physical concentration of the soul in one part of the body, a belief that the Igbos do not accept. This last point is clearly explained in the words of Benedict O. Eboh:

> The Igbos do not specifically identify the principal "seat" of the soul in man's body . . . the beating of the (anatomical) heart is one of the palpable singular signs and so they regard it as a principle of life. It is not, however, considered the "seat" of the soul as such, for although the heart is so closely associated with life, it is not believed to leave the body at death.[12]

From this it can be clearly understood that mkpulu-obi as a concept is deficient in conveying the Igbo idea of the soul for two reasons. First, it would lead to a localization of the soul in a particular area of the body. Second, it could suggest that the soul does not leave the body even at death.

Chi hypothesis: The concept "chi" is prompted by the view that man's soul is a resemblance of God. "Chi" as it is being used here means "life" in the sense of life from God, or the presence of God. The difficulty with this is the danger of what Westerners might call pantheism[13] because of the way *chi* has been variously used and understood among the Igbos. It is difficult to say whether "chi" means the life of God or life from God. The problem is hard to resolve because the two expressions *life of God* and *life from God* can be translated by one Igbo phrase ndu nke Chukwu.

However, I would think that "chi" is perhaps not too inappropriate for the soul, provided it is understood as not indicating that, for the Igbos, God is partitioned among his creatures. A major argument in support of the use of *chi* for the soul is that the Igbos have the idea that the soul in its activity directs and protects the body. "Chi," as an active participation of God in terms of life in man, would be correctly seen as directing the body.[14]

Muo hypothesis: According to this hypothesis the Igbo idea of the human soul is most appropriately conveyed by the term "muo," sometimes written as "mmuo." Basic to this term is immateriality. It is suggestive of that which is unseen in contradistinction to that which is seen. Muọ would be the most appropriate term that brings out the Igbo concept of the soul for the following considerations:

1. Muọ can be prefixed or suffixed to anything to mean the immaterial, spiritual or unseen component of that thing:

Muọ - madụ	:	a human soul
muọ - mụ	:	my soul
Arụ-na-muọ	:	body and soul.

2. Muọ cannot be located in a particular area of the body, and may not even be confined to one body, yet it can be regarded as the spiritual counterpart of a material body.

This exposition will help us to see how the theory of duality may help to understand the Igbo idea of the soul–body unity in man. It is not infrequent that the Igbos seem to speak of the soul as having the external appearances of a body. Yet in some areas, the soul is sometimes represented as having the size of a grain of sand. Its dimensions are so reduced that it can pass through the smallest crevice or finest tissues.

> This shows that its form is essentially inconsistent and undetermined; it varies from one moment to another with the demands of circumstances or according to the exigencies of the myth and the rites. The substance out of which it is made is no less undefinable.[15]

From this one can understand that if we apply the theory of duality to man, it will be observed that whereas the Igbos posit that man is made up of material and immaterial elements, they think of the soul, which is the immaterial element, as having obscure external appearances. They even go so far as to think of the muọ (soul) as having physical needs; it eats, drinks, hunts, etc. Yet the substance out of which it is made cannot be defined. This is because the people do not seem to be sure how to characterize the spiritual component of man. This uncertainty apparently renders any possible determination of the unity of soul and body in man in Igbo thought impossible. It appears that the soul is distinct and independent of the body, for during this life it can leave it and come back. This is evident from the fact that when a person suddenly faints or goes into a coma, the Igbos say that he has gone to answer a query before the council of elders in the spirit-land (ojeri ikpe ndi muọ). If he is exonerated he wakes again; if not, he never comes back to life. People who have gone through this experience sometimes talk about the persons they saw (perhaps known to some members of the community) who acted as the devil's advocate against them. When the exonerated person regains consciousness, the Igbos maintain that the person's soul that had wandered away has come back. From this one may conclude that for the Igbos the soul, although it is not located in a particular part of the body, is not bound to be always united to the body. It can leave the body without necessarily entailing death. Thus we see that the theory of duality, if it is maintained in a sharp sense, renders the soul entirely separate from and independent of the body. This would certainly pose an insolvable problem regarding the unity of the soul and body in man.

But this may not be the case if the theory of duality is considered in a inverted sense. According to this, as we noted earlier, the expression "ife ya na ya yi" considered in an Aristotelian sense of "that by which something is" indicates that the invisible element is distinct from and yet is in the physical part of a material object. In other words, in a spiritual sense the Igbos are talking of the invisible as if it is distinct from the visible. But in the metaphysical sense they show that the invisible world is not totally different from this world. Thus in the spiritual sense the soul is distinct from the body. But metaphysically the soul is in the body and is united to it. So one can say that the Igbo theory of duality maintained in a sharp sense leads to an impasse with regard to the question of the soul–body unity in man. But when the same theory is consideered in an inverted sense it seems to handle the problem.

The fact that the Igbo notion of the soul is obscure may not be surprising because it seems to be only a logical consequence of the people's way of life, which is characteristically practical rather than theoretical. The tendency is to express even spiritual concepts in a material fashion. But when these concepts are not expressed in a clearly materialistic mode, their expression often shifts from the materialistic to a quasi-spiritual expression which further confuses the matter. This problem is, of course, acute when you are dealing with spiritual concepts, obviously not with material concepts. The Igbos are definitely sure of what a material object is and of what it is made. This will be evidenced in the following Igbo theory of what makes a thing-to-be.

Ife-Melu-Ife-Ji-Di
The Igbo theory of
what makes a thing-to-be

In the course of my research work I had the chance to talk to Mazi Ede Oje, a typical Igbo elder, the oldest man in Ubogu, a village in Akpugo Nkanu of Anambra State. He was well over 100 years old. He could hardly stand even when propped up by his walking staff. Having lived through many generations, he is a link between the great ancestors and the present. He is an 'nze,'[16] an embodiment of traditional wisdom, a link between the past and the present. I had several discussions with him during my field work. Among the many things I observed about this man, one was that whenever I asked him a philosophical question, he insisted on sitting on a black, smooth-topped, stool-like piece of wood that had every sign of having survived many generations. It was beautifully smeared with dark colored blood. When I asked him what it was, he replied: "Nke a bu oche ndi gboo, oche ndi Nze, oche amamife, omenani." ["this is a stool of the past, stool of the representatives of the dead, a stool of traditional wisdom."]

Then I asked: "Why do you always want to sit on it before answering my questions?" He laughed and said:

Nwam, ajuju gi gbasalu : omenani n'ebe omiliemi. Yabu, kam wee zata ya ofuma odi mkpa nam ga anolu n'oche ndi Nze, kam n'ekwu onu fa n'ekwu uche fa. Oburo n'ike akam, obu omenani.	My son, your questions are concerned with tradition in its depth. So that I may be able to answer well, it is necessary that I sit on the stool of the representatives of the dead, to be able to speak their mouth, to speak their mind; it is not of my own authority, it is the tradition.

At this I decided to make that stool the center of our discussion. So I asked: "Kedu ife melu oche Nze a ji di?" (What made this stool of the representatives of the dead to be?) He peered at me without uttering even a word for some time. I figured that it might be that he did not understand my question. But his response later showed that he understood it at a deeper level than I had intended. He said that my question should be reframed thus: "Kọwalụ m ife nine kpatalụ oche Nze a ji di" (Explain to me all that contributed to making this stool of the representatives of the dead be.) His reason for reframing the question was that the first seemed to be concerned with only one side of the question. But the second was comprehensive enough to elicit the correct answers he was to give. When I accepted the reframing of the question, he then proceeded to give the answers:

Ife melu ochea ji di bụ : ife kpatalụ ojiri bụlụ ife ọbụ.	What made this stool to be is that which is responsible for its being what it is.
Fa di ụzọ ife anọ na eme : k'ife ọbụna bụlụ ife ọbụ.	There are four groups of things that make anything be what it is.
Nke mbụ, ife ana afụ : anya we ike imetụaka.	First, that which is visible and can be touched.

At this juncture he pulled out the stool from under him, touched all parts of it showing that all the visible components of the object come under this first group of things that make the stool what it is. He then continued:

Nke ibua, nke zolu ezo, : ọbụ ọdina ife na muọ. Ọbụ ife m ji malụ na ife a bụ oche ndi Nze.	Second, that which is hidden. It is that which is in the object in an invisible manner. It is that by which I know this is the stool of the representatives of the dead.

Then I wanted to know how that second thing comes together with the first. He said that prior to the process of the wood taking the shape it has now and carrying the smeared blood and other traditional decorations, the invisible was not in it. But as soon as the wood (material object) gained the shape, hardness, smoothness, size and other properties, as soon as the whole stuff could be defined as what it is, namely as "oche ndi Nze" (stool of the representatives of the dead), the first (visible) and the second (invisible) have met.

He still proceeded to give the third and fourth:

Nke atọ, onye nka, onye : Third, the artisan who used
ji osisi na ife ndi ọzọ wee   wood and other materials
lụta o che a.   to make this stool.

Nke anọ, ife kpatalụ eji : Fourth, the thing that
lụa oche ndi Nze a. Ya bụ,   brought about why this
ulu ọbalụ, ife melu ife ji di.   stool of the representatives
Nkea bụ nke kachasi mkpa   of the dead was built. That
n'ime ife inọa.   is, of what value it is, the
                            reason why a thing is. This
                            is the most important of
                            the four.

From these answers it is clear that in Igbo thought there are four
things that are involved in the process of the coming-to-be of any
sensible object:

1. Ife ana afụ anya : The visible and
   na emetu aka   tangible

2. Nke zolu ezo : The hidden (invisible)

3. Onye nka : The artisan

4. Ife kpatalụ : The purpose

These are the four principal elements in an Igbo theory of what
makes a thing to be. The first and second need no further explanation since they flow from the Igbo theory of duality already discussed.

Of the third element, I wish to observe that it is not identical
with the object in the process of coming-to-be. It is always external
to it. If we go back to our illustration of the origin of fire, it is evident that the object coming-to-be (the fire) and the sender (the head
of the inhabitants of the world of the unseen) are completely different.

Another significant aspect of this third element is that for the
Igbos, the Onye nka (artisan) of any material object can be seen in
two ways, either as visible or as invisible. This is because the people
have a basic conception that the process of the coming-to-be of any
object, be it material or immaterial, is mediately and ultimately the
work of the inhabitants of the unseen world. Here I will explain the
force of the two terms, mediately and ultimately.

Mediately brings out the idea that in the act of the coming-to-be of any object, the head of the inhabitants of the unseen world mediates between the artisan and the object under production. This comes from the basic notion that any dynamic action must be prompted by the suprasensible. In Igbo thought, dynamism is an essential property of the suprasensible (the divine.) Hence, an Igbo carpenter, even though he has all the tools, knowledge and art to produce a chair, when asked what he is doing, usually says: "I am trying to know if Ndi Muọ (the inhabitants of the unseen world) will give me their helping hand so that I can produce a chair."

Ultimately refers to the creative power of the head of the inhabitants of the unseen world. He is the ultimate source that sets a thing in motion. In the Igbo mentality it is ultimately from him that all ability comes, even the ability of the artisan to produce an object. Hence, the Igbos say that the process of the coming-to-be of any object has its ultimate source in Him.

The Purpose of matter

The fourth of the four elements that make a thing-to-be is so important that it is sometimes regarded as the sum total of the four elements. In the daily parlance of Igbo, the expression "ife kpatalu" can refer to the totality that makes an object in question to be. It also refers to the specific purpose of the object. For the Igbos, the purpose of a thing determines its being. In fact, whatever has no immediate, specific purpose is regarded as worthless. Its being is questionable.

By the purpose here is meant that use for which a thing is made. What purpose does it serve? If something new is presented to an Igboman, one of the most obvious questions he must ask is: "Kedu ulu ọbalụ?" (Of what use is it?) From the use he reasons back to the validity of its being. If it is of any use, then it is worth being.

Here it must be admitted that the ordinary Igbo may not reflect to this point of sophistication. However, the point we are trying to make is that in the Igbo way of considering objects presented for the first time, questions about it are essentially pragmatic.

For a Western reader, the Igbo analysis of causes has its resonance in Aristotle's theory of the four causes. The Igbos, of course, do not make use of these familiar Western categories but they are not talking about something totally different from Aristotle's own experience. Even the Igbo idea that purpose as the fourth element in what makes a thing-to-be is the most important of the four causes has its parallel in Aristotle's idea of the final cause as principal.

The important message we may take from the Igbo theory here

is that Igbo thought recognizes the universal question involved, namely: that of how a material object moves from a state of non-being to a state of being.

Critical reflection

As we come to the end of this chapter let us turn our attention to some of the merits and demerits of Igbo thinking. We have seen that the theory of duality as applied to the problem of the universals treats the latter at least in an embryonic form. In the question of the soul–body unity in man the theory, if maintained sharply (that is, sharp duality), would lead to an impasse. However, as we observed, the inverted version of the theory of duality provides a possible solution. The question still remains: Why is the Igbo idea of the soul hazy? In other words, why do the Igbo seem not to be very articulate about the soul?

I think that two major reasons could be offered for this. First, the Igbos tend to confuse the soul with external invisible forces. This is obvious from the fact that traditional Igbos speak of the soul as seen among the branches of trees. Thus B. O. Eboh writes that according to the Igbo traditional philosophy:

> When it [the soul] flutters among the branches of trees, it causes
> rustlings and crackings which even profane ears hear. But at the
> same time, magicians, or old men have the faculty of seeing souls.[17]

The rustlings and crackings caused by hidden birds and animals, or a sudden occurrence of a tropical whirlwind, can be understood by the traditional elders as the fluttering of the soul.

The second reason why the Igbos are not very articulate about the soul seems to be that they are not consistent in their idea that the soul is immaterial (at times they think of it in terms of a being with physical needs—eating and drinking—like human beings; at other times they think of it in terms of an invisible force. Consequently it is difficult to draw a clear picture of the nature of the relationship between the soul and the body). But I think that the real reason behind this is the problem of language. We cannot discourse of the "spiritual" without using words with material connotations. Not until Igbo metaphysics develops to a stage of critical reflection will this problem of language cease to be encountered whenever the Igbos are dealing with immaterial concepts.

One would say that one of the merits of Igbo thought as we have seen it so far is its attempt to explain the origin of material things. Here the Igbo mentality joins with the Christian traditional idea that everything in the material world was created by God, the head of the inhabitants of the world of the unseen. However, we cannot definitely say that the Igbos arrived at this notion from a solely philosophical point of view. It could have been a consequence of their religious inclination to accept everything that they cannot understand as coming from God. They cannot understand everything about the process of the coming-to-be and the ceasing-to-be of material things. But because they have a total religious outlook, instead of looking for the secondary causes they easily have recourse to God and accept the fact that the origin of material things must be traced back to the world of the unseen where Chineke (God the creator) creates everything. We shall see more of the Igbo idea of creation in chapter five.

Fundamental to the Igbo notion of purpose as the justification of the existence of material things is the Igbo concept of nature. In the Igbo language the word "nature" can be rendered in two ways: first, "Udi," second, "Ife de ka e si ke ya." Uodi is universal in scope in the sense that it is usually prefixed to a noun, for example:

| Udi madu | : | man's nature |
| Udi nkita | : | the nature of a dog |

to mean the essence of, the genus and specific difference of, something. In this sense everything comes within the meaning of udi because everything: man, animal, plant, spiritual being—has its own genus and specific difference. Here there is no difficulty in seeing how the concept of nature can be fundamental to the Igbo notion of purpose as the justification of the existence of material things. If the nature of a material thing means its essence, its existence can only be justified by its fulfilling the purpose of its essence, that is, being true to its essence.

However, a problem arises when we consider the Igbo concept of nature in terms of "Ife di ka e si ke ya," literally meaning, that which is as it was created. It was in this context that E. Obiechina observed that:

> ... the (Igbo) traditional world view ... implies a mystical utilitarian outlook on nature instead of an externalized appreciation of it in forms like fine landscapes, beautiful flowers, cascading waters or the colours of the rainbow.[18]

"Utilitarian outlook" obviously refers to the usefulness of the things of nature. The beauty of a flower is seen not in isolation but in and through its inner meaning, that is, its purpose. An Igbo thinker does not admire the beauty of a tree as it first appeals to the external senses. He goes beyond the sensory appearances. The attractiveness of the tree means little or nothing if it is not seen in and through its reality, a reality that is primordially value-oriented. Hence, if you speak to an Igbo person thus: "Hey! Osisi nkea amaka!" (Hey! What a beautiful tree!), his immediate reaction will be to retort with a question: "Kedu ife ọdi mma ya?" (To what purpose is its beauty?) How is it to be valued? Does it provide shelter with its green leaves, or food for animals or fruit for human beings? For such trees that do not provide either for animals or humans, the tone of the question will be: What does that tree signify? That is, is it a symbol of any of the inhabitants of the unseen world, a symbol of any of the virtues, such as justice? Is it in accord with the traditional order of things?

That the Igbos have a value-oriented idea of nature is patent. But the basic problem is that this idea of nature is one-sided. It is limited to the things that are as they were created. These would exclude all things that have been the products of human ingenuity: products of science and technology and the like. Considered more critically, the Igbo idea of nature excludes almost everything in our highly technologically developed world.

That the Igbos have such a limited way of understanding the concept of nature could be traced back to the fact that the traditional Igbo makes his daily living and carries on his daily activities in a natural environment that is little altered by modern technology. Consequently the Igbo idea of nature hardly compares with the Western concept of nature that we find in great minds like Aristotle who, in his formal division of the sciences, restricted it as an object of technical philosophical study to mobile things.[19] This means in practice that Aristotelian nature in a strict philosophical sense was limited to things that undergo sensibly perceptible motion. A mobile thing requires two components, matter and form. On the level of natural philosophy, the observed fact of change needs explanation through these two components. For Aristotle, each of them is "nature," and the composites to which they give rise are accordingly "things constituted by nature."[20]

From these considerations we get a clear picture of what nature comprises for Aristotle. Nature includes in its scope all things of the visible and tangible universe. To that extent it coincides with the ordinary, contemporary conception. The world of nature is readily understood to be the world we see and hear and feel around us, a world that is in endless motion from the gyrations of the tiniest particles to the tremendous outreaches of receding galaxies. The two conceptions of nature, the Aristotelian and the modern, thus coincide in scope and could imply that the Igbo idea of nature seems very inadequate.

However, I think that the reason for this apparent inadequacy of the Igbo idea of nature could be that the Igbos, like all traditional peoples of Africa, are "akin" to nature—and thus the difference between the Igbo and the Aristotelian ideas is basically that the Igbos lack the abstractionism requisite for the modern Western views of nature. As we shall see in the next chapter, this lack of abstractionism will also be noticed throughout our interpretation of the Igbo understanding of being.

Review Questions

1. "The question of the origin of the visible world does not seem to pose a serious problem for the Igbos." Do you agree or disagree? Give arguments in support of your position.

2. Produce arguments to show why the existence of the invisible world is an accepted fact among the Igbos.

3. State and exemplify the Igbo theory of duality. Show how it is an Igbo way of dealing with the problem of universals.

4. Use the philosophical problem of the soul–body unity in man to illustrate the merits or demerits of the Igbo theory of duality.

5. Highlight the similarities and dissimilarities between Igbo analysis of causes and Aristotle's theory of the four causes.

6. Give arguments to show why the Igbos are not very articulate about the soul.

chapter four

An Igbo understanding of being

In the last chapter we have seen that Igbo thought attempts to deal with philosophical issues in embryo, for example, the problem of universals, the soul–body unity in man and the question of causality. As we begin this chapter, we should note that a similar phenomenon may be observed permeating the Igbo awareness of the question of being.

Accordingly one should expect a number of discrepancies, lacunae, and perhaps inconsistencies and apparent contradictions in the development of Igbo thought in this and subsequent chapters. Our intention is to try to straighten out these where possible through an interpretative reading of the Igbo mentality. That these discrepancies exist should not be construed as undermining the quality of this work, but should be regarded as indicating the merits and demerits of Igbo metaphysical thought as it is in its present stage of development.

In this chapter the focus is on an Igbo understanding of being. According to the Igbos, one may derive a notion of being from the concept of man. Before we see how this is done, it is necessary to consider the concept of being in the Igbo language.

The Concept of being in the Igbo language

The Igbo language has no word that exactly translates the English word "being." However, there are two hypotheses with regard to what term approximates·the Igbo concept of being. These are the "onye hypothesis" and the "ife hypothesis." In the course of my field work I discovered that many of my informants favored the "onye hypothesis."

Onye hypothesis

The word *onye* is used in the Igbo language in three ways. As a pronominal adjective it means *who*, as in the clause: "Larry *who* is here" (Larry onye nọ ebea). As an interrogative adjective "Onye" can stand alone or be used to introduce interrogative statements. "Onye?" means "Who?" "Onye ma echi?" mans "Who knows tomorrow?"

Onye can also be used as a noun. In this category, its nearest but not exact English equivalent is *person. Onye* in this last sense is used to refer to living entities, both human and superhuman. A characteristic of this word is that even when it is used as a noun, it normally precedes an adjective or another noun. For example:

Onye ọzọ	means	another person
Onye nzuzu	means	a fool
Onye mmụta	means	a scholar
Onye nwe	means	Lord, owner
Onye Okike	means	creator
Onye uko	means	intermediary

At first sight it would seem appropriate to use the word *onye* for the Igbo concept of being. This is because it unquestionably conveys the idea of a human being and it can be employed to designate spiritual beings. Even when used in an interrogative form, there is no question that it can be used for the Igbo notion of being, whether human or spiritual. For instance, the question: "Onye melu ifea?" (Who did this?) can refer either to a human or to a spiritual being.

But the principal defect in using *onye* for the Igbo notion of being is that it cannot include inanimate, vegetative or non-human animate entities. In no way can one stretch the Igbo concept of "onye" to embrace things like stones, wood, or iron, etc. If, for instance, a piece of stone fell and broke a plate, an Igbo person would ask, "Onye kwụwalụ afele?" (Who broke the plate?) "Onye" here can never refer to the stone. What it refers to is *who*, the person who dropped the piece of stone that broke the plate. Hence, *onye* is not comprehensive enough to translate the term *being*. Let us consider the alternative hypothesis.

Ife hypothesis

The Igbo word *ife* primarily means *thing*, anything material or immaterial. It is also used to refer to a happening, an event, an occurrence. *Ife* can be affixed to any adjective or a verb to mean a specific
thing. For instance:

Ife ọbụna	means	anything what-ever
Ife ebube	means	a wonder, thing of wonder, a mystery
Ife mbelede	means	chance, accident
Ife nkiti	means	nothing
Ife ọjọọ	means	bad, evil thing
Ife ọma	means	good thing
Ife ma ife	means	the wise
Ife ama ife	means	the ignorant

According to the *ife* hypothesis, there is no other word in the
Igbo language that approximates the Igbo concept of being. I subscribe to this hypothesis for the following metaphysical reasons: the
Igbo notion of being is all-embracing, that is, it covers all categories
of being. As we saw earlier, whereas the concept of "onye" embraces
the human and suprahuman levels of being, it excludes inanimate,
vegetative and non-human animate entities. *Ife* primarily refers to
inanimate entities like the English word *thing*. But by an expansion
of meaning, it can be used to designate human and suprahuman beings. For example, when the traditional elder asks the question:
"Kedu ife kelu madụ?" (What thing created human beings?), any person conversant with the language knows that "Ife" in this question
refers to Chineke, the Igbo name for the highest of the suprasensible
beings, the unmade maker of all beings.

One of my informants, Mr. Benedict C. Emejuru of Ihiala, an
exponent of the "ife" hypothesis, in his effort to demonstrate that
ife is also used to denote human beings asked me the following
questions:

"Kedu ife melu njọ n'ụwa?" (What thing made evil in the world?
or What is the root of all evils in the world?) I answered, "Ego"
(money). "Kedu ife melu Ego?" (What thing made money?) I answered "Madụ" (human beings). Note that "ife" in the first question

refers to an inanimate entity, money. But "ife" in the second question refers to the human.

What is evident from our presentation here is that the Igbos readily use the concept "ife" in a particular sense to mean "thing," that is, inanimate being, and in a universal sense to mean any being at all, material or immaterial, inanimate or animate, human or nonhuman. I endorse the use of *ife* as the most appropriate word employed among the Igbos to express the Igbo concept of being.

However, we must note that *ife* does not bring out completely all that *being* means. *Ife* does not emphasize the important aspect of *being*, namely, the fact of existence. *Ife* standing on its own can be used to refer to both existent and nonexistent entities. Hence we have to search for a way of using *ife* to highlight the fact of existence and exclude the possibility of nonexistence.

The solution to the problem is in sight when we remember that *Ife* can be affixed to any adjective or to a verb to mean a specific thing. The Igbo verb *to be* in the sense of *to exist* is *idi*. *Idi* used as an adjective can be suffixed to any thing to show that it exists, for instance:

Okwute-di :	The stone that exists
Osisi-di :	The tree that exists
Nkita-di :	The dog that exists
John-di :	John who exists
Chukwu-di :	God who exists

In like manner idi can be used with ife to mean anything at all that is in existence. A combination of *ife* and *idi* in the modern Igbo orthography should be written thus: *Ife-di*. Ife-di is the most appropriate Igbo rendering of the English concept of being because it covers all entities, both visible and invisible, as well as the note of existence which we commonly associate with being.

The Categories of Ife-Di

Basic to the Igbo metaphysics are the categories of "ife-di": (a) the suprasensory category, (b) the human category, and (c) the thing category, that correspond to the diverse kinds of beings. Within each category are subcategories. In the suprasensory category are: Chineke and "Ndi muo" (the unseens). The human category is also subdivided into "Ndi di ndu" (the living), and Ndi Nwuru" (the dead). The thing category runs into three major groupings:

1. *Anụ*, literally translated as *meat* but means more than that. Here *anụ* is used to mean animals as distinguished from human beings and from inanimate beings.

2. *Ife nkịtị*, literally translated as "thing ordinary." Under this category the Igbos classify all inanimate entities. This is further subdivided into "Ife nkiti nwelu ndụ" (thing ordinary that has life), that is, vegetative beings and "Ife nkiti e nwei ndu" (thing ordinary that has no life) that is, nonvegetative beings, for instance, minerals.

3. *Ogụ*, that is, beings that have no existence of their own. Their being depends on a collection or interaction of different things (ife nkiti) placed together. For example, when a medicine man "creates" out of different things put together some kind of harmful medicine, an ogụ comes into existence.

With these fundamental distinctions of Ife-di in mind, we shall concentrate on our development of the point raised in our introductory section, namely: that Igbo man derives a notion of being from his concept of himself.

Being and man's
understanding of being

A Notion of being
derived from the concept of man

Like the notion of the soul, the idea of being as such remains insufficiently clear in the minds of Igbo thinkers. However, the Igbo idea of what is follows the two-fold division of the universe: the visible and the invisible. The visible world is a world inhabited by two kinds of being: human and non-human.

Human beings are the principal focus of the visible world. The Igbos express this idea in their names[1] and proverbs, for instance:

Madụ-ka	:	Human beings are the greatest.
Ndụ-b'isi	:	Human life is the first.

Confronted with the question: How do you become aware of what is? the Igbo, it seems, would say that an awareness of what is could begin with an awareness of man as a visible concrete instance of what exists. A review of the answers to my questionnaire will support his assertion:

Q. 1.	Gini bu ife-di? :	What is being?
A.	Ife-di bu ife-di. :	Being is being.
Q. 2.	Gini di? :	What is?
A.	Ife· nine bu ife-di. :	All things are beings.
Q. 3.	Kedu k'isi malu na ife : di?	How do you know that beings are?
A.	Emegi ife ọzọ, amalum : 'nkea maka na madụ di, maka n' anyi di.	I know this at least from the fact that human beings are. We are.
Q. 4.	Kedu ụzụ isi ama ife bu : n'ife di?	How do you know what it is that beings are?
A.	Ofu ụzọ bu sita na ima : ife bu na madụ di (mma-di).	One way is by knowing what it is that man is.

It is interesting to note that the number one answer, "Ife-di bu ife'di," is a tautology, yet it brings out an important point. A tautology of this type is used by the Igbo elder to indicate that what he is talking about cannot be defined. Thus in saying that being is being, my informant was acknowledging the fact that being, even though it is a common concept, cannot be defined in the way ordinary concepts are defined. Here the Igbos would subscribe to what St. Thomas said in *De Veritate*, that being cannot be defined in the way essences are defined. We cannot, strictly speaking, form an essential idea of being. It is the most evident concept to which every other concept is reducible.[2]

This first conceptualization of being is almost wholly implicit, and any attempt at this level to formulate explicitly the content of this idea invariably produces tautology. Although we can say that being is what is, is what is real, and that reality is being, we have no grasp of the meaning of "to be" and "to be real." From the first answer of my informant, one can understand the Igbo mind struggling with the perennial problem of how to grasp what it is "to be."

Not knowing what to do, he states it in a tautological form. This is nothing but a way of over-simplifying being into an empty concept, a point Heidegger warns us against:

> It has been maintained that 'Being' is the most universal concept. . . . But the universality of 'Being' is not that of a class or genus. The term 'Being' does not define that realm of entities which is uppermost when these are articulated conceptually according to genus and species. . . . The universality of 'Being' transcends any universality of genus. . . . So if it is said that 'Being' is the most universal concept, this cannot mean that it is the one which is clearest or that it needs no further discussion. It is rather the darkest of all.[3]

My references to Aquinas and Heidegger show that the Igbos bear witness to the philosophical tradition of maintaining that being is not an essence and hence cannot be defined as an essence is defined, by genus and specific difference.

The second answer of my informant takes a step further: Ife nine bu ife-di (all things are beings.) This is a way, I think, of stating that the notion of being penetrates all other contents; hence it is present in the formulation of every concept. This is keeping with the view expressed by Bernard Lonergan:

> . . . the notion of being is unique; for it is the core of all acts of meaning; and it underpins, penetrates, and goes beyond all cognitional contents. Hence it is idle to characterize the notion of being by appealing to the ordinary rules or laws of conception. . . . Other thoughts result from some insight either into the use of their name, or into things-for-us, or into things-themselves. The notion of being . . . cannot result from an insight into beings, for such an insight would be an understanding of everything about everything, and such understanding we have not attained.[4]

The views of Heidegger and Lonergan corroborate the Igbo uncertainty at this point regarding a defined notion of being. In the Western tradition, dating from Aristotle, being is not an essence and therefore indefinable. Ideas of essences are formed by abstraction, that is, by leaving out of consideration nonessential characteristics. Because being encompasses the whole of reality, there are disputes within the tradition on how the concept of being is formed. Still, it is generally agreed that being is not a universal concept, for universals are "essential" concepts, predicated in the exact same sense of all that falls under the concept.

In the third answer my informant's idea takes a dramatic turn:

Q.   Kedu k'isi malu na ife di? (How do you know that beings are?)

A.   Emegi ife ǫzǫ amalum nkea maka na madụ di (I know this at least from the fact that human beings are) maka n'anyi di, (We human beings are).

In this statement the Igbo is suggesting that a notion of being could derive from our concept of man. If so, the question is: What is there in the Igbo concept of man that will respect both the diversity and unity of being?

What is common in all being is the act of existence. But how do we move to this common notion from a concept of man?

The Igbo word for man (the human) is "madu." Etymologically "madu" is a short form of mmadi (mma-di) "Mma" is the Igbo word for "good," "a good," or "the good." "Di" is from "idi," which as we have seen is the Igbo verb "to be." For example:

okwute-di'   :   The stone that exists
                     (is)
osisi-di'   :   The tree that exists
                     (is)

In like manner, a combination of "mma" and "di" that is, "mma-di," means "good that is."

From this exposition of the meaning of the word for man (madu), we discover that in man the Igbo is able to discern the notion of "good that is." At this point two important questions must be answered: First, how are we to understand "good that is"? Second, how far does this notion respect the diversity of being?

The Igbo notion of "good that is" must be understood in the context of creation. For the Igbos the notion of "good" is derived from divine creation. To say that man is the "good that is" is not to say that man is "good in se," for no one is "good in se" except God. This is made manifest in such Igbo expressions as: (a) "Sǫ Chukwu di mma ezie," that is, "Only God is good in the true sense." (b) "Onye di mma belu sǫ Chukwu?" a question which translated literally means: "Who is good but only God?" The Igbos share the religious idea common to many peoples that man's goodness is participated. Man is "good that is" in the sense that, having been created by God, he is a product of his maker and hence shares in the being of his maker, the highest good. Igbo names such as *Chi-amaka* and *Chi-bu-mma*, are used to express this idea that God is the highest good. *Chi-amaka* means that God is the maximum good. *Chi-bu-mma* means that God is the good.

For clarity regarding this matter, we must look into the way in which Igbos use the verb *to participate*. There are several ways in which the Igbo language can translate this English infinitive; but for our purposes here we shall consider the two most widely used translations, namely: *iketa n'ife* and *isolu n'ife*. The first normally conveys the idea of individuals who come together to share something which as a whole belongs only to the group. It belongs to each of those who share in it only insofar as one is a member of the group. This kind of sharing is evidenced in a traditional Igbo funeral ceremony. Usually the family of the bereaved slaughters one or more fattened cows as part of the ceremony. The meat from the cows is shared freely by all. According to custom, even though all can partake of the cow meat, no one can say that the meat belongs to him *per se*, that is, as distinct from his being part of the community.

Our second expression, *isolu n'ife*, which means literally *to follow others in something*, conveys the same idea. Its force is better demonstrated in the expression: "Akwu solu ibe gbaa nmanu," that is, "A palm nut that has no oil of its own gives out oil when it is treated together with other palm nuts." This proverb emphasizes that participation is a matter of community appurtenance, not individual or personal endowment. From this as from the first expression, "iketa n'ife" we learn that in the Igbo mentality whereas man shares in the being of God as "good that is," man is not "good *in se*."

The answer to the question how the notion of "good that is" respects the diversity of being can now be seen when the notion is predicated of not only man, but also other particular things, using our previous examples of "this stone," "this tree," and so on:

This stone is "good that is."
This tree is "good that is."

Looking at these judgments, we see that each has a particular—*this stone* or *this tree*, as subject, and the verb *is* as predicate. If we substitute the general pronoun for these subjects, our judgment can be stated generally thus: Something is "good that is." We note that this generalized statement of the judgment does not leave out the particularity of the individual objects. The existence of a being is what makes it a being. So the judgment, "Something is 'good that is'," respects that which makes each object a being and yet it can be applied to any object, and this application is possible on the basis that all things are created by God and hence the notion of "good that is" can be attributed to them.

From what we have seen so far, two very important issues are raised here. The first issue arises out of divine participation: is Igbo metaphysics a pantheism? The second issue is the problem of evil. The question of participation will be handled in chapter five, because a detailed treatment requires exposition of the Igbo notion of "Chi" in relation to the Supreme Being. The problem of evil is what must be tackled now.

The Problem of evil

Even though the Igbos regard being as the "good that is," they are not so naive as to believe that there are no evils in the world. The fact that all beings are good in the ontological sense makes the question of moral evil crucial. Hence the Igbos are also concerned with the perennial problem of moral and physical evil. The Igbo ontological position that all things are good because of creation presupposes two things: first, that God is the absolute good who causes the good in all beings; second, that God's very act of creating is synonymous with his act of causing good in what he creates. In other words, by the very fact of its being created, a creature is good in a participated sense. Hence the question: How is it that there is evil in the world, and such evil that it sometimes covers the horizon of man's consciousness with darkness and despair? If God, the supreme goodness, is the cause of all things and all things caused by God are "good," how do we explain disruption in the physical universe, jungles of beings preying on other beings, savage disorder in the face of order, human suffering in bodies ravaged and spirits torn, the destruction of man by man, the self-destruction of moral evil? This is the age-old question that has harassed great thinkers. St. Thomas articulated the problem in this way:

> A wise provider excludes any defect of evil, as far as he can, from those over whom he has a care. But we see many evils existing. Either, then, God cannot hinder these, and thus is not omnipotent; or else he does not have care for everything.[5]

The problem of evil involves not only the question whether God is really all-good, but even that regarding divine omnipotence. It may also involve a denial of the very existence of God. If God were all-powerful, all-good, and beings are, according to the Igbos, basically good because of their participation in the divine goodness, God would want to take away all evil and be able to do so. Since everyday experience testifies to the presence of evil in the world, God must not be either all-powerful or all-good. In either case He would not be God. For reasons such as these, some people, with Dostoevsky's Ivan Karamazov, have been led to deny the existence of God.

The problem of evil is as old as man. The modern progress in technology has created new resources like biomedicine that endeavor to eradicate physical evil. Notwithstanding, the problem of evil seems to grow more intense. It appears in the current preoccupation with anguish, guilt, nothingness, failure or despair. Let us examine this problem under the following headings:

1. An Igbo understanding of evil.
2. The cause of evil.
3. A possible reconciliation of evil with the goodness and causality of God.

An Igbo understanding of evil: Evil is a phenomenon common to all peoples of the world. It is present at all levels of being. Natural catastrophes mar the face of the world; animals survive at the expense of other animals; men suffer sickness and death; human beings sin against other human beings and against God. The question is: How does an Igbo understand these and other instances of evil?

To answer this question, we have to go back to the concept of "omenani" which we introduced in chapter two. There we noted that, for the Igbos, "omenani" is an inherited pattern of thought and action that is mysteriously in harmony with the totality of all that is. As a clarification of this, we must add that Omenani is a generic term for the body of Igbo socio-religious laws, customs and traditions passed from generation to generation and handed down to the ancestors from God, Chukwu, through the Earth-god. For the Igbos an evil is basically regarded as an offense against "omenani." Even natural catastrophes, and all sorts of undesired occurrences in the universe are regarded as evils because they disrupt the normal order of reality which is supposed to be preserved by "omenani."

Social offences are regarded as "aru," a pollution or abomination, since they infringe the laws of the Earth-god who is the guardian of morality and the controller of the minor gods of fortune and economic life. The Earth-god works with the dead ancestors to reinforce prohibitions and ritual taboos. A deviation from customary patterns of behavior, such as the alienation of an individual from the community and similar infractions of accepted norms, are regarded as evils since they defy "omenani."

Among the traditional Igbos evils that afflict human beings are seen as afflictions or illnesses that come to their victims as punishments from the ancestors, the guardians of law and order. These punishments are supposed to be the consequences of the bad actions of the human beings concerned.

Whether an evil is an offence against anyone or anything, whether it is an occurrence among the living, the dead or the gods, the Igbos see it as a removal of an aspect of the well-being and completeness of "omenani." For a better understanding of the Igbo idea of evil, let us return to our treatment of Igbo community. In chapter two we indicated that the Igbos attach much importance to the community. The central ideas of the community are man, love and brotherhood. From these we get a comprehensive idea of the Igbo sense of evil. Achebe, in a novel, wrote:

> He that has a brother must hold him to his heart,
> For a kinsman cannot be bought in the market,
> Neither is a brother bought with money.

>> Is everyone here?
>> (Hele ee he ee he)

>> Are you all here?
>> (Hele ee he ee he)

>> The letter said
>> That money cannot buy a Kinsman,

>>> (Hele ee he ee he)

>> That he who has brothers
>> Has more than riches can buy.
>> (Hele ee he ee he)[6]

Achebe uses this poem to indicate the Igbo attitude toward each person in his society. In it we see the depth of the value bestowed upon each Igbo by his or her community. Each person is loved and cared for as a brother or sister. The poem expresses an Igbo ethical principle that guides all to a mutual recognition and acceptance of one another. By this principle, material wealth and riches have been situated in their rightful and meaningful place, namely, as subservient to man who is himself invaluable. It is a principle that expresses the Igbo sense of hierarchy: a priority in their cultural values. The Igbo social philosophy derives from this principle. "In it," says Egbujie, "we have the foundation of the Africans' principal cultural virtue, namely, the virtue of love, since to 'hold to heart a brother' means to love him."[7]

It is in the context of this virtue of love that the Igbos, as well as many peoples of Africa, spell out the details of daily living. As a consequence of this the Igbos have developed a high degree of personal involvement with one another's concerns in the community. Consequently, deviance and alienation from the social order, not to say revolt, are held to a minimum in the Igbo culture. Every individual person in the society is so surrounded by the love, concern, care, understanding, and responsiveness of others that aberrations are infrequent. The individual adopts the principle of the squirrel who in an Igbo proverb has said:

Ibidebe akwụ nso ka eji :   To live closer to the palm
atataya ụso.   tree gives the eating of its
                            nuts a special flavor.

Accordingly the Igbo way of life emphasizes 'closeness' but not 'closed-ness.' There is a closeness in living because each person 'belongs to' others and in turn, 'is belonged to by' others. By adopting this life of 'closeness' or 'belongingness,' an Igbo becomes immersed in the culture's spiritual substance, love; and by love he acquires a fulfillment as a person beyond mere individuality. When, therefore, a person commits a societal or moral offense, he is in effect regarded as having severed himself from this closeness, thereby stepping outside, as it were, the spiritual substance of the culture and running the risk of not fulfilling himself as a person. This spiritual substance of the culture was the intended legacy of the ancients, the founders of the Igbo culture.

Here we may ask: What is the foundation of this intention? As was indicated in chapter three, the universe for the Igbos is a unified whole of visible and invisible. Each of the four empirical categories of the world, the mineral, vegetable, animal and human, forms a unit but only as a part within a larger whole. The organic whole of the visible world spiritually blends with the divine, invisible world to give the Igbos the ultimate whole of all life. It is this idea of all of existence made up of patterned wholes that gave the Igbo ancestors the rationale for viewing their human society as an entity that must be holistic. Accordingly, man must form a union in order to enter into communion with other men in order to safeguard his own existence. This was the intention of the founders of Igbo society. The cultural norm is, therefore, that each and every individual must go out and behave toward others in order to establish a union and maintain communion with other people. Failure to do this constitutes an evil both for the individual and the community.

Two cultural expressions: "Tụụ-fiakwa!" and "Madụ madụ ibeya na adigh mma!" are very often used to perpetuate this cultural norm among the Igbos. "Tụụ-fiakwa!" is an exclamatory sound made by an elder of the community. This sound is usually accompanied with an emission of spittle. It is evoked whenever an adult is detected as tending toward indifference by his or her want of love and concern for others. The spitting out of saliva that accompanies the sound is the Igbo symbolic way of denouncing and spitting away, the impending evil.

This gesture is immediately followed with the second expression: "Madụ madụ ibeya na adigh mma!" that is, "The man to whom other human beings are not good!" This exclamation implies that such a one must either correct himself or be unacceptable to the community. Another widely used proverb completes the picture:

> A kinsman who strays into evil must first be saved from it by all, then, afterwards be questioned on why and how he dared stray into it to start with.

The most important point here is that an evil, be it committed by an individual or a group, is the concern of the whole community. As we noted in chapter two, the community does not leave the delinquent in isolation. He is always recognized as an indispensable part of the whole. Yet the evil is not condoned, and the culprit is not hidden away or helped to escape. Rather, the whole community comes out to eradicate the evil.

From the Igbo idea of community, founded on love and brotherhood, it is easy to discern that for the Igbos any evil, physical or moral, even though personal, has a community dimension. An evil is considered such because it fractures the ultimate whole of life; it causes a break in an existential unity. If we accept that this unity of the whole is a good, then we can rightly say that the Igbos, like St. Thomas, see an evil as a privation of the good that should be present.[8] Hence the question suggests itself: How does this privation come about? In other words: What, according to the Igbos, is the cause of evil?

The cause of evil: In general, evils can be grouped under three categories, namely, physical evil in the universe, physical evil in man, and moral evil in man or any personal being. However, regardless of the category to which an evil belongs, the Igbos locate its proximate cause or causes within the realm of the evil spirits.

In traditional Igbo culture the principal elements: Earth, Water (sea), Air (wind), and Fire (sun), are deified because they are extensions of divine activity. Hence a consideration of the symbolism of the Sea God and the Wind God is necessary to understand the Igbo idea of the cause of evil.

The Sea God is the most feared of all the gods. When this god sends floods, both the lives of men and of crops are destroyed. When it sends too little or none at all of its water, the same calamity befalls all life. The special abode of the evil spirits is the sea. Hence the diviners, the fortune-tellers and the members of esoteric organizations devoted to occult phenomena, play a significant role in Igbo society because they commune with these evil spirits. They prescribe what sacrifices must be made by both private persons and the community. They know into what part of the sea a person must throw his or her sacrificial objects and in what areas a person must take a bath to rid himself of the machinations of the evil spirits. These are normally performed in the silent darkness of the night in an atmosphere of fear. The sea, symbolic of the immensity and the transcendental powers of being, elicits in the traditional Igbo, the feeling of awe and sublimity. Hence its import is its power to produce a consciousness and a sense of mystery surrounding the source of existence. I. I. Egbujie has observed:

> The sea is a paradoxical element—on the one hand, it instills fear and almost a psychological despair of any meaningfulness to human existence in the world; but, on the other hand, because of its unfathomable sublimity and unconceptualizable depths, it furnishes the Africans with a certain hope and belief in the meaningfulness and reality of human existence.[9]

The sea, to the Igbo, is a special cipher-script, a special language expressing the transcendence of being. It makes life acceptable by presenting it as a mixture of good and evil. Though the sea is the abode of evil, it is also a symbol of good, the reality of human existence.

For the Igbos, the wind symbolizes the power of 'wiping away' evil. The sacrifices made to avert and avoid a possible approach or subtle establishment of the evil spirits' union with a person is normally performed in an open space, especially at a crossroad where the Wind God will blow off the evil to a sort of "no-where-ness."[10] Hence the Wind God is the purifying power of the ritual itself: in a word, the power constraining the powers of the spirits. Consequently the Wind God provides the Igbo with the assurance that life is meaningful. The Igbo, therefore, does not run away from his situation so long as he maintains good relations with the good spirits and gods.

However, like the Sea God, the Wind God is also a paradoxical element, doing both good and evil. When it assumes the form of a tornado, it blows furiously and tends to knock down everything in its way, houses and fruit trees. These in their turn may cause more harm by striking straying animals or human beings. The Wind God can bring down, in an undesirable quantity, the rains which destroy houses, leaving many people homeless.

Like the Sea, the Wind is a mysterious god. Whereas the sky is the embodiment of all celestial beings, the earth is the embodiment of all terrestrial beings. But the Wind has a sway over both. The Wind God, therefore, symbolizes an all-embracing power of God over beings.

Our remarks concerning these two element gods, the sea and the wind, afford a comprehensive knowledge of the causes of physical evil in the universe. From what we saw in chapter three regarding the bad spirits as the 'tune-players' of misfortune, we know that the bad spirits are the agents that cause human beings to commit moral evils. However, there are also good servant gods. These are ready and willing to cause man to do good. Although these gods have a power over evil spirits, they respect the freedom of man and hence do not compel him to avoid evil and do good. Hence it seems most likely that the Igbos would subscribe to the idea that some moral evils are caused proximately by men themselves since they can choose to do evil by handing themselves over to the evil spirits.

Two basic things to be noted here are: first, neither of the element-gods causes evil alone. Each of them is also associated with causing good. Thus we do not have reason enough to conclude that evil is caused in the process of causing good. In other words, we cannot conclude from the foregoing that for the Igbos, evil is intended indirectly while good is intended directly.

The second thing we may note is that the element-gods and the evil spirits are the proximate causes of evil. But who or what is the remote cause or causes? We have enough reason to believe that God could be regarded as the remote cause of evils since he is the creator of both good and evil spirits, and the element gods are the extensions of his power. Granted this, the question is: How can we reconcile evil with the goodness and causality of God?.

A possible reconciliation of evil with the goodness and causality of God: It must be admitted that from our consideration of the element gods there is no clear indication regarding the Igbo idea of how to reconcile the fact that God who is all good could cause evil, at least remotely, by creating beings who cause evil. However, if we look back to our remarks on community and the Igbo holistic view of the universe, we can gain further insight.

The Igbos have a sense of reality that is hierarchically structured. Regularly an occurrence is considered not in isolation but in relation to its place within the hierarchy. The way the community treats the evildoer and his evil demonstrates this. The culprit is not abandoned in his evil. Rather, the community takes all the steps to eradicate the evil in order to safeguard the integrity and well-being of the whole. We have seen that for the Igbos there is a greater good in the whole, which is normally regarded as having some elements of holiness and mystery about it. The Igbos think of evil as something that is not what it should be, something that makes the whole, the unity of life in community, less than what it should be. The fact that the Igbos regard evil as the fracture of this whole indicates that for them evil as evil cannot be caused on its own, but can be caused only as part of the effort to preserve the unity of the whole. The Igbos express this in a widely used proverb: Mmadụ amarọ ụma eme (njọ). This is a way of saying that one does not go out of one's way to cause an evil on its own. The implication is that the evil occurs as part of the struggle to preserve the whole.

However, judging from our treatment of the causes of evil, we note that the idea that evil occurs as part of the struggle to preserve "the whole" cannot apply to all evils as they are known in Igbo culture. As we have observed, the three proximate causes of evils are the evil spirits, the element gods and human beings. Whereas it can be accepted that the evil a human being or an element god causes proximately can be part of the whole, it is impossible to accept this in the case of evil caused by evil spirits. The reason is that for the Igbos the evil spirits are regarded as totally bad and incapable of producing any good. Hence whatever they cause proximately must be completely evil and not a part of the whole.

As far as proximately causing evil is concerned, God cannot be said to be responsible since he is not an evil spirit, an element god or a human being. But God can be seen as the remote cause of evil because he is Chi-na-eke, the one-who-is-creating. As Chi-na-eke he is the cause of all beings. Thus the Igbos say:

Chukwu kelu ife nine
(God created all beings)

Chukwu bu isi mbido ife nine
(God is the beginning (cause) of all beings).

Since he is the cause of all beings, he must be the cause of the proximate causes of evil, namely, element gods, evil spirits and so on. Hence God can be said to be the remote cause of evil.

In what sense can God be the remote cause of evil? Can he remotely cause the evil simply as evil? Judging from what we have seen of the Igbo idea of the proximate causes of evil, we can conclude neither that God remotely causes evil as evil nor the contrary. This ambiguity arises from the fact that if we say that God, in creating the remote causes of evil, creates them not as evil but as good, the question remains: what of the evil spirits?

However, there is an explanation. For the Igbos the evil spirits were not originally created and designated as evil. They were originally created by God as good, like other creatures. But during the course of their existence they turned evil. For example, if a man who in his lifetime had confirmed himself in evil ways died, he would join the company of the evil spirits, who, according to the Igbos, are the causes of evil on earth.

Thus our ambiguity can be resolved: God created all things as good, including the evil spirits. So if he is seen as remotely causing evil because He created the proximate causes of evil, it must not be in the sense that He causes evil as such but in the sense that out of the good (the whole) He causes, evil comes as a part of it.

With this understanding one can say that, for the Igbos, a possible way of reconciling the presence of evil in the world with God's goodness and causality is to realize:

a. that God does not cause evil proximately;
b. even in the remote sense his causing of evil can only be in an indirect way since he originally created the proximate causes of evil not as evil but as good.

To recapitulate, we began with a search for a concept of being in the Igbo language. We came up with "ife-di" as the most appropriate concept because it covers all visible and nonvisible entities and includes existence, which is common to all beings. Even with this concept, as we noted, the notion of being still remains insufficiently clear in Igbo thought. However, an idea of the Igbo awareness of what is begins with an understanding of man as an instance of what exists. Hence we went on to analyze the Igbo concept of man as "good that is." Applying this to individual instances of beings, we were able to arrive at a generalized statement that enables us to make the judgment: Being is something that is, or "good that is." This is a general way of expressing the being of each individual as well as the common intelligibility of all beings.

A charge that might be levelled against the Igbo way of deriving a notion of being is that since the Igbo idea of goodness is a notion derived from the Igbo concept of man, it actually means that the Igbo awareness of being is restricted to man and hence does not cover all beings. This objection might be answered this way. The Igbo idea of goodness is not limited to man. The source of goodness is God, the supreme goodness. But the basis of any creature's being good is the fact of creation. Therefore, all creatures, insofar as they are created beings, participate in goodness. Hence the idea of goodness cannot be limited to man because it includes all things created, and all things created are good insofar as they participate in God.

In the next chapter we shall further study being with a view to discovering how far, according to the Igbos, man's light of reason can go in the understanding of being in its ultimate cause.

Review Questions

1. Show whether the author is justified or not in favoring the *Ife* hypothesis.

2. "An awareness of what is could begin with an awareness of man as a visible concrete instance of what exists." Evaluate critically the author's illustration of this position.

3. Show how the views of Heidegger and Lonergan justify the Igbo uncertainty regarding a defined notion of being.

4. How do you understand the Igbo notion of "good that is"?

5. That all beings are good in the ontological sense all the more raises the question of moral evil. Discuss this statement in the light of Igbo metaphysics.

6. Discuss the Igbo attempt at a possible reconciliation of evil with the goodness and causality of God.

7. Is the Igbo awareness of being restricted to man or does it cover all beings? Support your answer with one argument from text and one from outside the text.

chapter five

Being and God

In the last chapter we arrived at a notion of being as something that is. In the present chapter our aim is to discover what, according to the Igbos, can be known about being. This investigation will take us into the ultimate cause of being. But it will not end there. We will have to examine how the Igbos arrive at this ultimate cause. What is the relationship between it and its creatures? Finally, what does this cause mean to its creatures? Our discussion will be arranged in the following major sections:

1. From the Igbo holistic view of the universe to the Ultimate Cause.

2. The Existence of God (Chukwu).

3. The Igbo Knowledge of God.

From a holistic view of the universe to the ultimate cause

Here we present a view of the universe as the Igbos conceive and accept it, live in it, and behave in it as their cultural environment. The question is: What does the world mean to the Igbos? The principal meanings according to which the Igbos live their practical daily lives are the meanings they have extracted from the universe. These meanings give us the Igbo horizon of vision. Hence a careful analysis of these meanings should yield an understanding of the fundamental concepts, ideas, and principles of the Igbo culture, and hence a better understanding of the Igbo idea of being.

We shall in this analysis investigate further the clusters of meaning disclosed in the Igbo understanding of the chief elements of Earth, Water, Air and Fire as no longer purely material entities but as ciphers which reveal spiritual realms. In these realms these elements are deified and personified. Finally, we will display the symbolism of these beings to demonstrate that the Igbos' practical and symbolic views of the world embody their theoretical ones.

An illustration of this intimate link between the practical and theoretical understanding that exists in Igbo culture, as well as in other African cultures, can be found in Janheins Jahn's *Muntu*, who quotes Adebayo Adesanya:[1]

> This is not simply a coherence of fact and faith, nor of reason and traditional beliefs, nor of reason and contingent facts, but a coherence or compatibility among all the disciplines. A medical theory, e.g., which contradicted a theological conclusion was rejected as absurd and vice versa. This demand of mutual compatibility among all the disciplines considered as a system was the main weapon of Yoruba thinking. God might be banished from Greek thought without any harm being done to the logical architecture of it, but this cannot be done in the case of the Yoruba . . . since faith and reason are mutually dependent. In modern times, God even has no place in scientific thinking. This was impossible to the Yorubas since from the Olodumare (the god of the people) an architectonic of knowledge was built in which the finger of God is manifest in the most rudimentary elements of nature. Philosophy, theology, politics, social theory, land, law, medicine, psychology, birth and burial, all find themselves logically concatenated in a system so tight that to subtract one item from the whole is to paralyze the structure of the whole.[2]

Jahn has used this citation to support his thesis that the traditional African view of the world is one of extraordinary harmony. A similar view is also shared by the Igbos. Regardless of the fact that they believe in the existence of two worlds, the Igbos, like all Africans, have an extraordinarily harmonious view of the universe. This view is the basic criterion by which all things, including life itself, must be measured for their meaningfulness and cohesiveness.

Every institution of Igbo culture has this sense of unity as its foundation as well as its sustenance. This explains why, for instance, in Igbo kinship relations, a deep sense of unity underlies what anthropologists call an extended family system. In a holistic view of the universe, no one is ever seen or left in isolation. This is why among the Igbos, as well as all African peoples, everybody dreads the sanction of being ostracized from his community. This likewise explains why in Africa the cult of the dead is a widespread phenomenon, a cult which is at the same time an indicator of the strength of a people's historical consciousness.

We may ask how the Igbos arrived at this basic cultural concept. How is it that, according to the Igbos, to subtract one item of existence from the whole is to paralyze the entire structure? In other words, how do the Igbos understand existence and what fundamental meaning does the universe have for them?

To answer these questions we must understand that in the traditional Igbo religion, for instance, the Earth is a god and is worshiped daily. It is venerated as the Supreme Mother of all that exists. Moreover, as we saw earlier in chapter four, both the Sea and the Sun are also divinized; so is the Wind, to whom sacrifices are made to ward off evil spirits.

For the Igbos, existence cannot be questioned directly. It remains a mystery, an enigma. We see the grass, weeds and plants that were not there before sprout from the womb of the Earth. Thus the Igbos sense that the Earth enjoys the fertility whose generative force is the principal source of these new existents. But the Earth left to itself cannot bring these things into existence. The Earth's arid soil is of little avail. It needs water, whether the waters of the sea, river or sky. Thus, like the Egyptians[3], different Igbo communities have a special reverence for local rivers and lakes. Sacrifices are offered to them so that they may bring their waters in moderation to aid the Earth's fertility in yielding an abundance of crops. On the farms people prune off the leafy branches of trees which might shade from the direct benevolent actions of the sun's heat and the wind. Thus the Igbos see some unity in the functions of the four chief elements of the universe—Earth, Water, Air and Fire. It is through their combined actions that the crops which sustain humans are produced. Each of the elements needs the others so as to manifest and fulfill its own function. This fact is of profound existential import to the Igbos; from it the idea of the universe as an organic unity is formed. It is here that we have the origin of that holistic view of things. Such a view, according to Innocent Egbujie:

> gives us the ontology of Africa's basic principle of viewing the world itself and then the world of men as an internally related whole. It is an enduring African cultural principle because of the 'timelessness' of the source from which it has been extracted. For

these four elements of the universe never desist from their holistic function of introducing that which comes into existence in time. This explains why the Africans insist that to be human one must be at-one-ment with nature, the world and the universe.[4]

The question inevitably arises: How did the Earth with her power of fertility come about in the first place? Why should the Earth need the ancillary functional powers of Water, Sun and Wind in order to display her power of fertility? This brings us to the idea of causality that leads to the Supreme Being.

Causality

The Earth's fertility is an idea fundamental to Igbo cultural life. The Earth is a mother which feeds and nurtures people. The Earth did not endow herself with the power of fertility; otherwise she would not need the forces of the other elements. Whence, then, comes the Earth's power of fertility? Here the Igbo makes a spontaneous leap prompted by reason to a superhuman power. In this process reason and faith complement each other. It is in this leap and by it that we have the birth of Igbo traditional religion. That superhuman, super-sensible power is the Igbo God, Chukwu, the ultimate foundation of all beings. Chukwu, through the mediating power of the earth's fertility, a power with which he has endowed her, is the author of existence and all forms of life.

Igbo folk-tales recounting the origin of material things, for example, fire, as we saw in chapter three, are commonly used by the people to teach young children the fact that Chukwu is the source of all beings.

The "Gods"

We have arrived at Chukwu as the ultimate source of all beings. The Igbo mind's perception of the world does not stop there. Our earlier question was concerned with how the chief elements themselves came to be gods. The Igbo mind goes beyond the merely physical, the mere materiality of these elements, to their spiritual realm. Now we may ask: by what mental process or logic do the Igbos ascend to that sacred realm of the elements?

The answer is simple. According to the Igbos, as well as many other African peoples, the power of production is the only true power a being has. It is a power that the Igbos behold with awe because they see it as derived from the power of God in producing the world. God is sacred and commands man's veneration for he has created the universe and all things therein. The Earth has her native power of fertility by which she produces. She is therefore an extension of the divine activity. She is therefore a god, a servant-god to Chukwu. By the same train of thought, the Sun, the Sea and the Wind are gods. They are sacred by their own intrinsic power, albeit a power that is given. Thus we have, in the Igbo mode of perception, an earth which is no longer a purely material earth but in essence, a god. So is it also with the other elements.

The Symbolic meaning of the Earth-God

A question that arises from what we have said is: What for the Igbos is the symbolic meaning of the deification of the primary element, the Earth? The Earth, because of its fertility, is the archetype of all forms of maternity. It is the symbol of love because it "mothers" and cares for all things that exist. When the assembly of Igbo elders reaches a decision for their community, that decision and the course of action that it entails are usually regarded as "the word of the land." This is because the Earth symbolizes the common spirit, common agreement and the unified mind of the people.

Since the Earth is sacred by reason of her power of fertility, by extension the woman is sacred because she has a womb and the power of giving birth. But the Earth has a special mysterious power. It is at the same time both male and female since it is both father and mother at once; hence "father-land" is "mother-land."

The symbolism of the Earth has a special practical significance for the Igbos. An Igbo is truly himself when in his consciousness he is one with the earth. To be one with the Earth is to be one with the whole of reality. Thus, it is generally held among the Igbos that a normal Igbo does not dare betray the Earth. To do harm to another person, for instance, is to betray the Earth. The expression "to betray the Earth" for the Igbo means to commit an abomination against the Earth, the universal mother of all.

From this we can infer that the Igbos see in and through the Earth the provident hand of God. Through the medium of the Earth, God provides for us, his creatures. This providence is normative in that it prescribes the special African cultural virtue, namely, that of acceptance of everybody. This is the basis of the everyday symbolic prayer of the Igbos expressive of good will toward all, namely:

Egbe belu, Ugo belu, nke si : To perch on the ground oc-
ibeya ebena, nku kwalụ ya.   casionally and not to be
                              perpetually in flight is a

necessity to the life of both
the hawk and the eagle.
But should either of them
attempt to deny the other a
perching place, may its
wings wither off.[5]

Thus far we have seen how the functional unity of the elements
has provided the Igbos with the basis for their holistic view of things
and how within this milieu the people, prompted by reason complemented by faith, are able to discover God as the ultimate source
of all that is. From this arises a new question: Does God actually exist? This is the topic of our next section.

The Existence of God (Chukwu)[6]

Possible ways of arriving at the existence of Chukwu

The Igbos are not very much concerned about proving in a formal
way the existence of God. They prefer to say that the fact that God
exists is obvious. The immediate question is why is it obvious to
them?

Two reasons might explain this: the Igbo religious background,
and man's sense of dependence. These are interconnected. An Igbo
feels insecure when on his own, that is, without reference to higher
powers. This sense of insecurity naturally arouses in him a tendency
to seek shelter from superhuman powers who, in his judgment, are
strong enough to assure him maximum protection in every sphere
of insufficiency. These superhuman powers are the ancestors, spirits
and messengers of God. They are in constant communication with
human beings and make the presence of God felt as an unquestion-
able fact among the people. Apparently a typical, traditional Igbo is
in constant communion with God through these superhuman powers.
Thus he satisfies his religious inclination and strengthens his dependence on God.

The point here is that because the Igbo is born in a religious atmosphere that makes the presence of God a living fact, he has not
the least doubt that God exists. Consequently the Igbo normally
does not bother about a proof of God's existence. God is so near to
man, so involved in man's existence, that one does not question
Chukwu's existence. Mr. Ede Ani Onovo, a man well known for his

wisdom and knowledge, a native of Onuogba in Akpugo Nkanu, highlighted this idea in his responses to my questionaire:

Q.1.:	Onye bu Chukwu?		Who is God?
A.:	Chukwu bu "ndi muo" nwe ife nine, Okike kelu ife, Onye nwe ndi muo na ndi mma-du.		God is the "unseen" who possesses all beings, the creator who creates being, who possesses the unseen and human beings.
Q.2.:	Chukwu odi ezie?		Does God really exist?
A.:	Chukwu di ezie.		God really exists (is).
Q.3.:	Kedu ka isiri malu na Chukwu di?		How do you know that God exists?
A.:	Nkea nwolu ewu n' okuko anya. Asi na Chukwu adiro, Ife ahaghi adi.		This is obvious even to goats and fowls. If it is said that there is no God, then being would not be. Nothing would exist.
	Asi na Chukwu adiro, ndi Igbo agaghi na aza "Chukwu-di"		If it is said that God does not exist, the Igbos would not be answering *God exists* as a name.
	Asi na Chukwu adiro ndu agaghi adi.		If it is that God does not exist, there would be no life.
	Chukwu diri adi, Odifu, Oga na adilili.		God was existing, He is still existing, He will continue to exist.
	Nna nna anyi fa kwulu ya. Obu etua ka Ife is di.		Our great, great ancestors said it. That is how reality is.

Obviously in the above responses my informant has affirmed that the existence of Chukwu is so obvious that the question of demonstrability does not arise. However, a detailed scrutiny of his answers reveals some clues to possible ways of arriving at the existence of Chukwu:

> The existence of things of nature
> Igbo nomenclature
> The Igbo concept of Chi
> The Igbo idea of life and death.

Through the things of nature: "Asi na Chukwu adiro, Ife agaghi adi." ["If it is that there is no Chukwu, then being would not be."] This expression of my informant contains all that is required to construct a demonstration of the existence of Chukwu from the reality of the things we see around us. If there were no Chukwu, the source of beings, there would be no being. But beings are, that is, things are, since we perceive and experience them around us. Therefore there is Chukwu. In other words, the fact that beings are is a proof that Chukwu, the source of being, is.

Through Igbo nomenclature: "Asi na Chukwu adiro, ndi Igbo agaghi na aza Chukwu-di." ["If it is that Chukwu does not exist, the Igbos would not be answering *God-exists* as a name."] Igbo names express the reality of what is.[7] Some of the names, for instances, Chukwudi (Chukwu-di), Chukwudifu (Chukwu-difu), Chukwuno (Chukwu-no) express the reality of the existence of Chukwu. In Chukwudi, the operative word is *di* which comes from the word *odi*, the third person singular of the verb *idi* which, as we have seen, means *to exist*. The name Chukwudi therefore states unequivocally that Chukwu exists. Chukwudifu, is an emphatic form of Chukwudi. The addition of *fu* is to assure even the most critical mind that the existence of Chukwu is beyond doubt. Chukwuno brings out the fact that Chukwu is present. To be present, clearly, one must exist. Hence, the existence of Chukwu is a reality.

Through the Ibgo concept of Chi: Chi, as we are going to see in an analysis of the Chukwu concepts, is a participation in Chukwu. Human beings obviously do participate in Chi as the life of God, and in his daily life the Igbo experiences this participation.[8] Hence Chukwu is a reality. in other words, if the parts exist, the whole must exist.

Through the Igbo idea of "life and death": "Asi na Chukwu adiro ndu agaghi adi." ["There would be no life."] The pheonomena of coming-to-be and ceasing-to-be, of life and of death, are realities outside the control of finite beings. But they are undoubtedly happening everyday. Hence there must be some being transcending these phenomena who is controlling them. This way to the existence of Chukwu is based on the Igbo belief that nothing happens without a cause. If things are coming to be and ceasing to be, there must be a cause. But the phenomena involved are above human power since man is also coming-to-be and ceasing-to-be. Man has no comprehensive control over these. Hence for the Igbos, the ultimate cause of these movements must be located within the sphere of the unseen. In this sphere all original causes are attributed to none other than Chukwu who is Chi-na-eke, that is, the one who is creating.

Granted that through these ways we have arrived at the fact that God exists, we should note that up to this point all that we can say about him is that he is the cause of all beings. We still need to know more about Him. As a step toward this, we shall consider some of the ways of viewing Him among the Igbos.

Seven ways of naming Chukwu

Our brief discussion of the four possible ways to the existence of Chukwu brings us to another important aspect of Igbo theodicy, the ways of viewing Chukwu Himself. Some of these are:

Onye-okike: Okike comes from the verb *ike* which means *to create."* *Onye-Okike* therefore means *a Being who creates.* This is more profoundly expressed in the name *Chi-na-eke* (*Chi who creates*). *Onye-okike* and *Chi-na-eke* are specifically reserved for the Supreme Being who alone can make out of nothing, the maker of all entities. *Eze-chita-oke* (king or head of the phenomenon of creating) is another way of expressing this. These expressions highlight the primordial function of Chukwu as creator.

Okasi-akasi (The highest highest): This name points to the transcendence of Chukwu who is over and above the totality of all that is. He transcends all experience. He is afube (the like never seen), Onye-kasi-enu (Being who is at the topmost), Eze-igwe (King of heaven). The sublimity of this transcendence is depicted in a beautiful Igbo expression descriptive of Chukwu thus: "Exe bi n'igwe ọgọdọ ya n'akpụ n'ani": literally, a king who lives up in heaven with his garment touching the ground. This is an idiomatic way of saying that Chukwu is beyond the ordinary; he rises above heaven and earth.

Amama-amasi (known but never fully known): This expression shows the immeasurability as well as the incomprehensibility of Chukwu. Chukwu Ebuka (God is the greatest) also brings out the same notion. By these expressions, the Igbos indicate their belief that Chukwu can be known no matter how poor and imperfect our knowledge of him may be. On the other hand, they maintain that no matter how advanced human knowledge may be, we can only scratch the surface of our knowledge of him. No matter how intelligent man is, he is stupefied and even dumbfounded when he tries to comprehend Chukwu. Hence the Igbos say that Chukwu is Ogbalu Igbo ghalii (incomprehensible to the Igbos).

Ife-anyi (For whom nothing is impossible): This is an attribute portraying the all-embracing power of Chukwu. Even the impossible is possible for Him. Nothing escapes His wonderful power. *Ife-anyi* is part of *Ife-anyi-Chukwu,* a name given to a child born of a woman who had been regarded as barren for a very long period. Oka-ike (most powerful), Chi-nwe-ike (Chi who possesses power), Chi-debere (Chi who keeps all things as they are) are also expressive of the same reality, namely, the unrivaled power of Chukwu. Other expressions are *Olisa-bulu-uwa* (Lord who carries the world); *Omelu-k'okwulu* (who keeps to his words); *Onye-ana-ekpelu* (to whom prayer is directed); *Odenigbo* (whose fame resounds everywhere). This last one literally means he whose fame resounds in Igboland, but by an extension of meaning it signifies everywhere. Chukwu is everywhere present. *Onozu-ebe-nine* (present everywhere), *Chukwu-fuzulu* (Chukwu sees comprehensively), are other expressions showing that nothing escapes the all-knowing presence of Chukwu. This fact is clearly portrayed in the question: "Ina ezonari madu ibe gi, ina ezonari Chineke?", that is, "If you successfully hide from your fellow human beings, can you also do so from Chukwu?"

Eze-ogholigho-anya/Omacha (King of knowledge who knows all): These indicate the unfathomable depth of Chukwu's knowledge. He knows everything, even the impossible as well as the improbable. Other expressions in this line are *Chukwumacha* (Chukwu knows all), *Chinweuche* (Chi has intellect) and *Chi-ka-odili* (It belongs to Chi). These are indicative of the Igbo idea that Chukwu is the source of all knowledge.

Chi-gboo (Chi for ever): Gboo in the Igbo language refers to the very, very distant past, to time immemorial as well as "outside time." So

Chi-gboo asserts the eternity of Chukwu. This is emphatically stressed by another expression, *Chukwu-difu*, which has the connotation of: Chukwu was, is still and will continue to be. It is part of a longer expression: Odili adi, odifu ogana adilili (he has been, is still, and will continue to be.)

Eke-ji-mma (Creator who holds goodness): This depicts Chukwu as the Being who has the perfection of goodness. It really means that Chukwu is goodness. Other ways of expressing this idea in Igbo are: *Chukwu bu so mma* (Chukwu is but goodness); *chukwu-amaka* (Chukwu is superlatively good).

It is interesting to note that these different ways of viewing Chukwu are based on two basic presuppositions: first, that Chukwu actually exists; second, that Chukwu is the ultimate in any list of positive or beneficent categories. The onye-okike, for instance, is the ultimate in the list (series) of the categories of efficient causes. This is attributed to none other than Chukwu who alone can exercise the function of ike-ife (creating). *Ike-ife* literally means "bringing into being, originating or causing without preexistent material."

From this exposition one conclusion can be drawn: that the Igbo ways of viewing Chukwu find expression in the different names reserved exclusively to him. No other being can be privileged with such names. Among the Igbos, we noted, names are not considered as mere tags to distinguish one thing or person from another but are expressions of the nature and reality they signify. Hence as names these ways of viewing Chukwu are expressions of the significance of God as the ultimate cause of all beings. This introduces us to an important question, namely, what, in the mind of the Igbos, does God mean? In other words, is God, as the ultimate cause of all beings, simply an abstract notion, or has he real import for the Igbos? This is basically the question of the Igbo knowledge of God which will be handled in the following section.

The Igbo knowledge of God

The question of the Igbo knowledge of God arises out of the practical nature of Igbo philosophical thought. The Igbos, as we indicated earlier, are more practical than speculative in their manner of viewing reality. In our discussion of the purpose of matter in chapter three, we saw that the Igbos ask what practical purpose a thing serves. Similarly, the Igbos normally want to know what God as the ultimate source of all being means in a practical sense. The answer to this is what we shall explicate as the Igbo knowledge of God.

Of all the names by which God is known to the Igbos, *Chukwu, Osebuluwa* and *Chineke* are the most basic and the most commonly used. They are the most basic in the sense that all other Igbo names for God seem to derive from them. An analysis of the composition and the significance of these names will help us arrive at an understanding of what the Igbos know of God and what He means to them in a practical sense.

Our guiding question is: What do the Igbos mean when they pronounce the names *Chineke, Osebuluwa* and *Chukwu?* What ideas do these names connote?

Etymologically *Chineke* (Chi-na-eke) is a combination of three words, *Chi, na* and *eke,* which mean literally, "Chi who is creating." The expression *na-eke* (who is creating) in the Igbo language is reserved solely for that activity by which a thing is made out of nothing. Such an activity is well known to be the prerogative of the Supreme Being. *Na-eke* is never used in relation to man because man is not Onye-okike (the one who creates). In the use of this name, therefore, the Igbos express their knowledge of God as the creating God. The work of forming the entire universe, and all in it: the good and the evil, the visible and the invisible is continuously being effected or permitted by God. In this capacity, he is known as Chineke. From this derive all other names expressive of the creative activity of the Supreme Being, for instance, *Onye-Okike, Eze-chitoke, Chukwu-Abiam, Anyanwu-Eze-Chitoke.*[9] The operative word in all these names except Chukwu-Abiam is the verb "ike" which we have said previously means "to create." It also means "to share," "to divide," "to portion out." As C. Obiego observed:

> The underlying thought in these names is the idea of creation and in them God is considered as he who "portions out" something to creatures . . . NDU, the thing God "portions out" or puts into creatures is life.[10]

Some parts of Igboland use the name *Chineke* more often than *Chukwu. Ezechitoke* is the name used by the elders mainly in parts of the Nsukka Division. However, it is rapidly falling out of use.[11] It depicts God as "the chief of creation." *Chukwu-Abiam* and

Anyanwu-Eze-Chitoke are mainly liturgical usages, especially in sacrificial rites. The former portrays God as "the creator of everything, the creator who comes to clearer light as he portions out life.[12] *Anyanwu-Eze-Chitoke* indicates that God as the creating king is identified with the sun that rises and sheds light on all beings. Permeating all these names is the idea of the continuous activity of God. We shall seek to discover what this continuous activity means for the Igbos. But, before we do that, let us consider the meaning and significance of the name *Chukwu*.

Chukwu (Chi-Ukwu) is from two words *Chi* and *Ukwu*. *Ukwu* means "biggest," "supreme," "highest." *Chukwu*, therefore, means *highest Chi*. Then what does *Chi* mean? In retrospect we see that *Chi* is common to all the names we have so far used for God. Hence we can suppose that it is an important concept in Igbo theodicy. So we must ask: What does it originally connote for an Igbo?

Foreign writers, as well as indigenous researchers into Igbo religion, have treated this concept in different ways, ranging from those who take chi to be a "spirit" or "monad" to those who say that it is a "kind of group-self or multiplex-ego able to manifest itself in several individualities at the same moment."[13] Some have even taken this to be the individual's guardian angel. Thus Ọnụọra Nzekwu declared:

> Chi, according to our traditional religious doctrines, was a genius,
> a spiritual double connected with every individual's personality.
> Every individual has a Chi, a guardian angel.[14]

Simon Okeke stated that "the duty of the personal chi can be compared with the duty of angel guardians for Christians."[15] Chi has also been likened to the Egyptian "Ka": the double or genius of a man, an ancestral emanation which guided and protected him during his lifetime and to which he returned after death.[16]

These attempts are laudable as pioneering efforts but I would hesitate to accept any of them as the philosophical meaning of Chi because each of them is either deficient in conveying the original meaning of the concept or compounds a philosophical error.

Chi cannot mean the *guardian angel* because the idea of a guardian angel came to the Igbos only with Christianity. It completely defies the imagination to accept Chi as an ancestral emanation since this would indicate that the concept has nothing to do with God. To believe this is absurd since it is the basic concept in practically all the Igbo names for God. Talbot's idea that chi is a "monad" which exists outside of man or "a multiplex ego" would inevitably lead to the belief that the Igbos have a polytheistic notion of God, which actually they do not have. Indeed, this claim would be contradictory to the Igbo concept of Chukwu which means "the highest Chi." There can be only one highest Chi, otherwise it would not be the highest ("Chukwu ama bụzi Chi ukwu").

To pinpoint the exact meaning or connotation of the Igbo concept of chi is not easy. This is due to the particularity and the universality of its dimensions. Chi in its particular connotation is reserved to the Supreme Being. But considered in its universality, it is found in all beings. Here, of course, we are confronted with the question: If chi, which is reserved to the highest Being, is also found in all beings, does it mean that the Igbos have a pantheistic notion of God?

As a prelude to a treatment of this question, it is important to bring in the Igbo concept of life (ndu). The Igbos have a tremendous respect for life because life is very precious, indeed priceless; something that only God can give. Hence the Igbos say: "Ndụ k'akụ," that is, life is greater than wealth. An analysis of several Igbo names, *Chibundu* and *Chinwendu*, will lead us to a deeper understanding of *ndu*.

Chibundu is an abbreviation of "Chi-ukwu-bu-ndu" (Chi-ukwu is life). This name contains an ontological assertion, for it equates the being of Chi-ukwu with that of ndu. *Bu* is from the Igbo verb *to be*, which expresses identity. Chi-ukwu, as we have shown earlier, expresses the idea of the highest Chi. But there cannot be two highest entities in the same category. Only one Chi-ukwu is Chi-na-eke (Chi who creates).

Chinwendu is an abbreviation of Chi-ukwu-nwe-ndu (Chi-ukwu has life). This means Chi-ukwu to whom life (ndu) belongs absolutely. Chi-ukwu is the author or source of ndu. From here the true meaning of Chi in the Igbo mentality comes to light. Chi as the source or author of life is life itself. So *Chi-ukwu* is Ndụ-ukwu, that is, the *Big Life* (literally), absolute life. This is another way of saying: Chi-ukwu is pure existence, the necessary Being from whom beings derive their being.

The issue here is how we can understand the Igbo idea that "Chi" which is first and foremost reserved to God is also found in creatures.[17] In the light of what we have seen so far about "Chi," let us take the names *Chi-na-eke* and *Chi-ukwu* respectively and consider them in relation to creatures.

The Name Chi-na-eke

Chi-na-eke, as we saw earlier, means *Chi-who-is-creating*. Note that it does not simply mean *Chi-who-creates*. This would mean that Chi creates a being and is finished with it once and for all. Rather, Chi-who-is-creating conveys the notion of a here and now present cause producing an effect. Here lies the clue to the philosophical meaning of Chineke for the Igbos. The idea of God as the creator is closely connected with presence. An Igbo scholar whose work comes closest to indicating this is C. Obiego. In an effort to explicate the theological meaning of Chineke he wrote:

> ... Our sentence would be "Chi-is-creating...," in short, the creating Chi, Deus creans. This is the popular and normal way of understanding the word in Igbo society. "Chi-Is-Creating" voices out the idea, namely, that creation is a continuous activity.[18]

When the Igbos speak of Chi as being reserved to Chineke and found in creatures, they mean that God, the source of "ndu" (life), is here and now producing "ndu" in creatures. The Igbo concept of "chi" therefore indicates the continued presence of the cause in its effect. The presence involved here is what Martin Buber referred to as a kind of pre-conscious presence, an ontological union in being.[19]

The key to understanding how the Igbo idea of chi can apply to the relation between Chi-na-eke and the beings of experience, is grasping the fact that the relationship involved here is causal. Since causal activity takes place in the effect, an agent is always joined immediately to its effect. This can be seen in experience; for my hand must be joined to a pen in order to cause it to write. The immediate effect of Chi-na-eke is the "ndu," that is, the existence of the beings of experience.[20] Hence Chi-na-eke as the cause of beings is present to every being. He is joined directly to each as cause is joined to effect. Thus we can say that as long as a being has being, God is present (Chi na eke). This interpretation, even though not explicitly expressed, was suggested in the theological work of C. Obiego:

> Chi is continually creating, i.e., his creative activity is believed to be constantly at work. Hence he is called in this respect Chukwu Abiama: for, as for the Igbo, every manifestation of the forces of nature proves to human experience that these forces are not static nor are they mechanical and as such they need the continuous and continuing activity of the creating Chi.[21]

It is this "continuous and continuing activity of the creating-Chi" that we interpret philosophically as the metaphysical presence of God in creatures since his causality, present in effects, constitutes the very being of creatures. It is an ontological union of being which is the basis of the existence of the beings of experience.

This interpretation suggests that the Igbos join with the Western tradition in the view that:

> Since God is being itself by his own essence, created being must be His proper effect as to ignite is the proper effect of fire. But God causes this effect in things not only when they first begin to be, but as long as they are preserved in being; as light is caused in the air by the sun as long as the air remains illuminated. Therefore, as long as a thing has being, so long must God be present to it, according to its mode of being. But being is innermost in each thing and most fundamentally present within all things, since it is formal in respect of everything found in a thing. Hence it must be that God is in all things and innermostly.[22]

To affirm that God is in all things and innermostly is to state that he is present in all things by his power and by his essence. As all things are in His power, His presence extends as far as his causality. Whenever he is present, he is present wholly, that is, essentially, because there is no composition in God. It is this presence of God in creatures that the Igbos call *chi* (with small letters), that is, "chi" found in the beings of experience. This is obvious from the way they speak of "chi madụ" (a man's "chi") as a guiding director of a man's life. Man's fortune is determined by his "chi." A man who is successful in life is described as one whose "chi" is alive and active. Very often the following expressions are used among the Igbos:

Onye chi ya mụ anya,	He whose chi is
ife nine ana agalụ ya.	awake, all things work
Onye chi ya lapụtalụ,	well for him. He
nke ya agwụsia.	whose chi betrays, is
	finished.

The presence of God in and to his effects is not to be understood as a material presence since God is immaterial. The Igbos express this thus: "Chukwu bụ mụọ." His presence to his effects is therefore not subject to the limitations of material presence. It is an intimate presence, an innermost presence. This can be seen from the fact that his presence in the creature ("chi") is the very act of existing ("ndụ") which he causes in the creature. But this act of existing is what is innermost in each being. Hence God is at the heart of every being as the being's chi. He is more intimate to each thing than its own self. All this is summarized in the one name, Chi-na-eke, that is, Chi who is creating.

When we say that God is intimately present to each creature, we must remember that this is a presence grounded in causality. But since God causes the existence of the other as other, he is fully present without being part of the being he causes, and his effect is not part of him. Here we see that even though chi in the Igbo sense is found in all things, it does not necessarily mean that the Igbos have a pantheistic idea of God.

From these considerations, the answer to our original question regarding what the Igbos know of God through the name *Chineke* is clear; namely, through this name the people express their knowledge of God in the practical experience of life. God is a God who is present among us, and his presence means life for us. This provides an excellent ground for refuting the erroneous doctrine which maintains that the God of the Igbos is a "high God, which is also a sky God. But he is often a withdrawn high god, a *deus otiosus*."[23]

This, of course, has been strongly refuted by scholars like A. Shelton and B. Idowu who have shown that the God of the Africans is a living God rather than a withdrawn high god. Anent the idea of asserting a withdrawn high god for the Africans (and hence for the Igbos), Professor Idowu[24] made an interesting remark: namely, that if ever there were a god who is a figment of man's imagination, it is this high god. For he is only an academic invention, an intellectual marionette whose behavior depends upon the mental partiality of its creators.

A little familiarity with Igbo culture quickly reveals the creative presence of God among the people. Their frequent allusions to the effects of God in their daily lives are constant reminders of this fact. In the next section we shall see that in Igbo culture this creative presence entails care and support in creation.

The Name *Osebuluwa*
(God's care and support for creatures)

In the last section our analysis of the meaning and implications of the name *Chineke* has enabled us to gain some insight into God in his relation to his creatures. We have seen that the relationship is not a notional one. It is chi, the most intimate metaphysical presence of the creator in the created. At this point we want to know whether this presence entails for creatures more than their being.

That God's presence to his creatures is metaphysical means that God is not to be conceived as a vast, inert, static being. He creates and he is actively present in all that he creates. God is a living God, an active God. Among the Igbos this is usually expressed thus: "Chukwu di ndụ" (God is living). The Igbos also utilize this as a name in an abbreviated form: Chukwudi, or Chidi.

Since God is living and active, his presence in creatures must be manifest in some activity of their daily lives. This activity is expressed in one of the Igbo basic names for God, *Osebuluwa*. Etymologically this term comes from three words, *Olisa* (or *Ose*), *bu* and *Ụwa*. *Ose* is used among the Abuchi people to represent a deity carrying and supporting the world on its back. The Igbos, especially the Onitsha area people, use *Olisa* for the Great God. *Bu* or *bulu* is a verb indicating a *carrying, supporting hand*. "*Ụwa*," as we already know, means *the visible world*. Looked at together, "*Ose (Olisa)-bu-uwa*" indicates the *Great God carrying*, supporting, and hence providing for, *the world*.[25] *Aka-Olisa*, a derivation from *Olisa-ebulu-uwa*, is used among the Igbos to mean the *provident hand of God*. *Osebuluwa*, therefore, as a name for God indicates that the Igbos recognize that God has a plan for the world and he supports and directs his creatures to a realization of this plan.

In his research work C. Obiego confirmed that the Igbo name, *Osebuluwa*, and other names related to it, suggest a deep rooted conviction of sustained divine providence:

> . . . they (the Igbos) call the "creating-Chi 'Osebuluwa' "—"He who is carrying or supporting the world," including man; and were the creating Chi to release his hold, the world would relapse into "nothingness" (Ife obuna adeghe na ụwa).[26]

Providence, from the Latin *providere*, literally means *to see beforehand*, or *to plan for*. It implies not simply a causing in general, but one that comes from a practical knowledge about an action to be performed in order to reach some end. The practical knowledge here involves two things: first, a plan and, second, its execution. Providence applied to God in this sense involves his knowing plan for each creature and for the universe as a whole, and his carrying out of this plan, his directing of creatures to their ends. With the idea of "Chi" in Igbo culture, it is easy to conceive of God as directing every creature to an end since the concept of "chi," as we have seen, indicates the people's belief that God is ontologically present in every being. But a question that may arise is: How do we know that every creature has a tendency to an end? In other words, is there anything, either concept or occurrence, in the Igbo culture that points to the fact of final causality in the sense of an order-to-an-end for the entire creation? The answer should be positive if we recall the Igbo notion of omenani. In chapter two we defined the Igbo concept of omenani as an inherited pattern of thought and action customarily and mysteriously in harmony with the dynamic creativity of being within the totality of all that is. In this definition we already anticipated the answer to our question.

Among the Igbos omenani is not just like the English idea of tradition. Tradition as an inherited pattern of thought or action may or may not be actually in use here and now depending on whether one decides to follow the tradition or not. But Igbo omenani has an eternal binding force in the sense that it retains in the present the force it had in the past and there is no sign that it will lose this force in the future. The expression in our definition "mysteriously in harmony with the creativity of being" points to the fact that omenani for the Igbos will continue to retain its force as long as there is being.

The spirit of omenani (that is, the compelling urge to act according to what is acceptable within omenani), is a dynamic force that pulls all creation together. How? Earlier in this chapter we saw how the Igbos have an extraordinarily harmonious view of the universe from the functional unity of the four elements—Earth, Fire, Water and Air. This harmony is maintained as part of the observance of the stipulations of omenani. This is evident from the way the people regard any event that betrays a tendency to break out of this harmony. For instance, if the Sky fails to provide water at the right time for the Earth to give life to crops, it is regarded as "Alu," that is, an abomination against the Earth-god, and such an abomination is seen as "going contrary to omenani." What that means is that the Sky has failed to act according to its end. From this we know that there is such a thing as a final end for the elements. In Igbo culture this end is expressed as "Ka esi eme ife, Odi na ani," that is, "being in harmony with omenani."

The idea and practice of community living in love and concern for each other which we explain in chapter four have as their focal point being in accord with Omenani. "We are our brothers' keeper," is the social philosophy commonly practiced not only among the Igbos but also among all Africans. To go against this constitutes an infringement of the demands of Omenani. A familiarity with the Igbo way of life reveals that there is a general tendency as well as an inner urge in all beings of experience "to dance according to the tune of Omenani."[27]

This general tendency and inner urge constitute what I think is a strong indication of the order-to-an-end we have been discussing. To a Western reader this may sound strange and unconvincing. But to an Igbo who has an experience of the spirit of Omenani, it will not because he can easily understand the impact of my expression "to dance according to the tune of Omenani." For the Igbos, an individual who has successfully danced according to the tune of Omenani all his life dies a good death and is united with the good spirits, the ancestors, who are united with the Creator from whom they get the power to protect their families here on earth and serve as the guardians of Omenani.

Thus we can say that in Igbo culture the spirit of Omenani is an indication of the reality of an objective order in the universe. In this order everything is directed to its particular end on the one hand, and fits into God's total plan for the universe on the other. The validity of this conclusion is grounded on an Igbo popular proverb: Awọ ada agab ọsọ efifie na nkiti. Literally this means: "A frog does not run during the day for no purpose." But understood culturally this proverb says unequivocally that there is a final order in creation.

Also, the Igbo concept of Osebuluwa testifies to this order. That God does not only create for an end but even supports, directs and guides his creatures to that end is highlighted by the import of the verb *bu* which, as we have seen, indicates a continuous action. If God is supporting, directing and guiding the whole creation, it must be to a goal, otherwise his action would be in vain, which is absurd. There must therefore be an end to which His action leads.

From this it is clear that Igbo culture recognizes the fact that God who, as Chi-na-eke creates and is actively present in His creatures, as Osebuluwa has a plan for each creature and an objective plan for the entire creation and guides and supports them to this end. Thus the active presence of God in the beings of experience means His care and support of these beings to the realization of their purpose. Concisely, Chineke is Osebuluwa.

From our reading of the significance of these two names, Chineke and Osebuluwa, we have gained some idea of the Igbo knowledge of God in relation to his creatures. A knowledge (no matter how imperfect) of God in relation to his creatures certainly demands an inquiry into a knowledge of what God is in Himself. This knowledge will constitute the focal point of our next section.

The Name Chi-ukwu

Chi-ukwu is the name by which the Igbos express their knowledge of God as he is in himself, apart from any relation to creatures. It is an absolute name. As we have seen earlier, *Chi-ukwu* means the *highest Chi.* Here we must add that God for the Igbos is not the highest Chi in the sense that he is the topmost on the list. He is the highest in an absolute sense, that is, in that he is a being who is totally other. The Igbos express this idea in a very commonly used dictum: Onye di ka Chukwu? Who is like God? They also answer this as a name, Onyedikachukwu (sometimes abbreviated as Onyedika).

Through the medium of this saying put in a question form the Igbos want to convey the idea that nothing is like God. He is entirely different from everything and everyone else. God transcends all boundaries. He is the Chi-gboo, the aged but not aging Chi, that is, the eternally existing Chi whose existence is incomparable to anything conceivable by human intelligence. The otherness of God is emphatically highlighted in an Igbo expression: Chukwu-di-eqwu, that is, God is lofty, sublime and incomprehensible. He is transcendent.

Since God is the highest in an absolute sense, He is the unlimited fullness of being, the Supreme Being. Taking *Chi* as *life* (ndụ), we see, *therefore*, that *Chi-ukwu* thus expresses a knowledge of God as the *fullness of life*. Through this name God is also seen as a being whose perfection is not received; for if he received any perfection, he would not be an unlimited fullness. His perfection is boundless in its transcendence. To be for him is just to be, simply and absolutely.

The Problem of Participation: An important issue that arises from our consideration of the name Chi-ukwu is the question of participation. If God is the fullness of being, the unlimited fullness of perfection, how is it that beings are? To put it in the Igbo way: if God is Chi-ukwu, how can anything else be? We have put off this question until this point because here it can be addressed directly. It will help to put into perspective all that we have been saying of God as he is in himself and in relation to creatures.

The question is more penetrating than it looks at first sight. It involves seeking a reconciliation of the principal ideas that the Igbos express concerning God through the names Chineke, Osebuluwa and Chukwu. If we remember that Chineke indicates God as the Creator who is actively present in his creatures; that Osebuluwa highlights him as caring, supporting and directing beings to the end he has for them; and that Chukwu refers to God as he is in himself, the fullness of being; the question can then be posed: How can God be Chi-ukwu and yet be Chi-na-eke and Ose-bulu-uwa? That things are is because God is Chi-na-eke and Ose-bulu-uwa. At this point it becomes evident that our question is as fundamental as Parmenides' metaphysical question: If there is Being, how can there be anything besides?

The last form of our question takes us to the celebrated fundamental question of philosophy: If there is something how can anything else be? This is what Kierkegaard called

> the miracle of creation, not the creation of something which is nothing over against the Creator, but the creation of something which is something.[28]

The last section of this quotation calls for our special attention. "Something which is something" is something over against its Creator who is Chi-ukwu, the absolute ground of all being. This "something" is something, that is, it truly is, yet it is grounded in Chi-ukwu, an is which transcends it.

As Robert L. Hurd has shown in his article in *Listening*, Kierkegaard's "miracle of creation" is best illustrated in

> the human subject who is pre-eminently something of its own, something autonomous and yet still dependent on another.[29]

The "miracle of creation" viewed in Igbo terms would be that God who is Chi-ukwu has created beings (the human subjects, for example) who are something of their own, that is, autonomous; and who, as participants in God seen as Chi-na-eke and Osebulu-uwa, are still dependent on another. Here our original question—How can God be Chi-ukwu and yet be Chi-na-eke and Ose-buluwa?—shades off into one of the key concerns of modern and contemporary philosophy, namely, the question of human autonomy. So our problem of participation is hereby narrowed down to the problem of human autonomy, that is:

> the strange possibility whereby Absolute Being [Chi-ukwu] allows for a free, autonomous being over against itself (the possibility of created or contingent freedom).[30]

The problem of human autonomy or human freedom in Igbo metaphysics becomes obvious when we recall our earlier discussions of the Igbo concept of omenani. There is a general tendency and an inner urge in Igbo culture, as we noted, to "dance according to the tune of Omenani." This indicates that in Igbo culture God as Osebuluwa guides and directs individuals and the community to an end He has chosen for them. The issue is then: How can a human person (the most self-possessed of created beings) be his own and yet depend on the Absolute Being who guides and directs him? How can we reconcile these two things: distinctness from Chi-ukwu in the sense of autonomy, and beholdenness to Him precisely in the act of autonomy?

It must be admitted that in the history of philosophy some thinkers, for instance, Feuerbach, Marx, Nietzsche and Sartre do not see any possible reconciliation. For them the human subject must seek "birth through himself"[31] as an absolute will-to-power, absolute self-invention and freedom. The human subject should and must be ontologically autonomous. According to them, to reach self-fulfillment man must step out of the realm of beholdenness to God and enter into the realm of absolute being-in-itself. This means, of course, becoming God. As we are going to see shortly, the Igbo mentality would differ from this extreme position and would rather attempt a possible reconciliation.

The Igbo attempt at a reconciliation of autonomy and independence: From the Igbo idea of community we know that the people's cultural life is characterized by love, concern, brotherhood and a deep sense of belonging. These characteristics give rise to a general adoption of cultural norms. They also constitute the basis for the general tendency and the inner urge to "dance according to the tune of Omenani." In this context, it would seem, especially to Western readers, that the general adoption of cultural norms do generate a generic kind of cultural communication in which everyone acts, believes and thinks alike. The fact is that opinions, fears, joys and goals are imperceptibly transferable from person to person because of such an original, unquestioning identification of all. From this it would seem that by living in such a community, the lucidity of one's self-consciousness is veiled and therefore one is not yet in a completely realized communication since one is not yet aware of autonomous selfhood or will. In such a community it could appear as if each person is reduced to an ego point which is substitutable for another mere ego point. This can be illustrated by the fate of Obi Okonkwo, the chief character in Chinua Achebe's novel, *No Longer At Ease.*

The gist of the story is that Obi Okonkwo was sent to England for a university education sponsored by the contributions of his town's people. Having imbibed Western culture, he came back to Nigeria and found himself oscillating between two cultures, his people's culture and that of Westerners. The crux of the problem was his personal decision to marry a woman whom he met in England. Virtually all of his town's people were opposed to this marriage as we can see from the following citation:

> 'Very good,' said Joseph bitterly, 'Are you going to marry the English way or are you going to ask your people to approach her people according to custom? . . . What you are going to do concerns not only yourself but your whole family and future generations. If one finger brings oil it soils the others. In the future when we are all civilized, anybody may marry anybody. But that time has not come. . . . What is an engagement ring? Our fathers did not marry with rings. It is not too late to change (your decision). Remember you are the one and only Umuofia Son to be educated overseas. We do not want to be like the unfortunate child who grows his first tooth and grows a decayed one.[32]

During one of the monthly meetings of the Umuofia Progressive Union, Lagos Branch, the president spoke on behalf of the entire town to Obi:

> 'You are one of us, so we must bare our mind to you. What the government pays you is more than enough unless you go into bad ways.' Many of the people said: 'God forbid!' 'We cannot afford bad ways,' went on the President. . . . You may ask why I am saying all this. I have heard that you are moving about with a girl of doubtful ancestry, and even thinking of marrying her. . . .'[33]

In view of all these remonstrations, Obi had to withdraw his decision to marry the woman of his choice. This would show that in the Igbo community no one may freely choose whatever he decides. Thus it seems that the Igbo society does not accommodate the freedom of an individual who wants to have his or her own way. However, it is important to remember that, as we saw earlier, the principal Igbo cultural norm is that 'one should so act as not to bring afflictions to the entire society of which one is a dynamic part.' This principle presupposes and recognizes each person's free capability for deviance.

> It is a principle (says I. I. Egbujie) underpinned through and through by freedom itself. Since the Africans' sacred holistic view of . . . the . . . world . . . put together is such a strong existential ideal, how could an African society come to let a member of its human world go his or her own way, a thing which would be tantamount to the polluting of the whole?[34]

Implied in this citation is the belief that for Africans the freedom of the human subject is better respected within the context of the whole. Thus the insistance on the individual's adherence to the entire community, rather than being a hindrance to one's freedom, is really designed to facilitate the good use of one's freedom, especially insofar as one's interest is basically involved. No law commands anyone to love himself. But since unrestrained love of self is bound to implicate others, those others rightly rebel against purely egotistical conduct.

One thing we must admit here is that the Igbos are dealing more with the question of a practical, a cultural phenomenon within a society, than with the metaphysical examination of freedom. In the latter case any consciously deliberate human act derives from freedom, and is an index of freedom. Freedom abstractly considered admits of all possible and imaginable individual decisions and choices even to the point of the option not to choose, which is itself a choice and proof of freedom. On the other hand, in practical freedom, since no person alone makes up a community in which a culture inheres, there is the ongoing dialectic of the individual's freedom and the societal freedom that originally produced and conserves cultural norms. The logic, then, of the Igbo community is that since it has been the free decisions and choices of the forerunners of the community to establish a free bond that was passed on to posterity, it is not proper for one to decide abstractly against those meanings and realities thus handed down.

> According to the Africans there is no such thing as freedom's reason to negate freedom in the practical order. It is still within one's free self-articulation that one chooses to unite with primordial freedom's constitutions, the substance of a culture.[35]

So it is among the Igbos. For them one's free self-articulation is meaningless unless it is within the context of the community's freedom. Notice that "to unite" here is not the same as merely to conform. Conforming is not truly the attitude of a free agent because of its externality. But the attitude of uniting is truly that of a free agent since it reflects what is fundamental to a human being living in a society.

From the foregoing we may gather that the Igbo idea of freedom of the individual seems to be like the Christian idea of freedom: individual freedom is not freedom to kill or destroy oneself (otherwise it would not be a sin to commit suicide), but freedom within the provident hand of God guiding and directing to the final end. In fact, one is most free in a reasonable sense only when one is free in this context, which actually is the context of creation. To be free outside this context means that one was not created.

The delicate dialectic of the individual's freedom and the community's freedom is analogous to the dialectic of the part and the whole in a sentence. The whole which is the meaning of the sentence transcends each word, its part. The words manifest their meaning only in the context of the whole. Yet the role of the part cannot be minimized. Similarly, a respect for the freedom of the whole does not minimize the freedom of the individual.

Clearly, unlike more individualist cultures, the Igbos have not lost sight of the community as the primordial basis of an individual's freedom. This totality of the community is what is symbolized by omenani. But omenani, as we saw earlier, is symbolic of the Absolute—Chi-ukwu. With this understanding it is evident that the Igbo way of reconciling the two ends—human autonomy on the one side and beholdenness to an Absolute on the other—is to see the latter as the ground of the former. Human autonomy can be authentic only if it is grounded in a beholdenness to an Absolute from whom it derives its meaning. We have seen this amply demonstrated in the Igbo cultural milieu. To think of an autonomy in terms of Sartre and his forerunners would be a contradiction in terms in Igbo culture. The ground of such an autonomy would be nothingness, so there would be no autonomy at all. For the Igbos there is either an autonomy grounded in beholdenness to an absolute or no autonomy at all.

The very fact that the Sartrean project logically leads to the absurdity of making the human subject an absolute, that is, a god, testifies to the validity of our point. Practical experience would show that it is just not possible to have the human subject become an absolute being, for this would mean having as many absolute beings as there are human subjects. If all human subjects are absolute, the result is that one is still compelled to go beyond these absolute beings in search of the ground for them. Then a more fundamental question has to be asked: How are we to define *human*? In other words, how do human beings perceive themselves? Are we absolutely autonomous in religious experience?

To recapitulate, throughout this chapter we have sought for an understanding of being in its ultimate cause from the Igbo point of view. We have seen how the functional unity of the elements has provided the Igbos with the basis for their view of things. Within this milieu the people, prompted by reason complemented by faith or religious understanding, discover God and accept his existence as the ultimate source of all that is.

From that point our focus has been on what, according to the Igbos, we can know of this God. Our consideration of Igbo names for God has been of help to this. The major names are *Chineke*, *Osebuluwa* and *Chukwu*. *Chineke* introduces us into a knowledge of God as the *ultimate source* of *being*, the creator who maintains a causal relationship with all beings. This causal relationship is expressed in the Igbo concept of "chi," a most intimate metaphysical presence of God in each of his creatures. From our analysis and interpretation of the significance of the name *Osebuluwa*, we understand that this creative presence of God entails his care and support. God's presence in creatures means that he has a plan for them, and directs and guides them to the achievement of this end.

A consideration of the implications of the name *Chukwu* led us to realize that even though God is intimately and creatively present in his creatures, the Igbos still recognize that this God, as he is in himself, is the unlimited fullness of being, the Absolute who is totally "other," that is, distinct from all his creatures. From this arises the issue of participation which we saw as the problem of reconciling the Igbo ideas of God as Chi-na-eke and Ose-buluwa on the one hand and Chi-ukwu on the other. An examination of this issue led us back to the primordial metaphysical question asked by Parmenides: If there is Being, how can there be anything else?

In the light of contemporary philosophy the question was seen as that of Kierkegaard's miracle of creation: the creation of something which is something. But this miracle, as Hurd has shown, can be narrowed down to the contemporary problem of human freedom. Hence our chapter ends with the Igbo way of viewing or reconsidering the problem of the autonomy of the human subject and beholdenness to an Absolute Being; namely: seeing the latter as the ground of the former.

In the final section of this work, attempts will be made to highlight the problem of Igbo metaphysics, the impact of this metaphysics upon other areas of philosophy, and some of the practical results of the Igbo understanding of being as we have presented it in this chapter and the preceding chapters.

Review Questions

1. Show how there is a movement in Igbo thought from a holistic view of the universe to the ultimate cause.

2. "The fact that God exists is obvious." Discuss.

3. Present a critique of the possible ways of arriving at the existence of God.

4. Discuss the seven ways of viewing Chukwu as an important aspect of Igbo theodicy.

5. Drawing out the metaphysical import of the names, *Chineke, Osebuluwa* and *Chukwu*, present a critique of the Igbo knowledge of God.

6. Explicate the term *Chi* as an important concept in Igbo theodicy.

7. The idea of God as the creator is closely connected with presence. Discuss.

8. Using the name *Osebuluwa*, show what it means to say that God's presence in His creatures is metaphysical.

9. The spirit of 'omenani' is a dynamic force that pulls all creation together. Show how this is an indication of the order-to-end in Igbo metaphysics.

10. What does it mean to say that *Chi-ukwu* is an absolute name? How does it give rise to the problem of participation?

11. How does Igbo metaphysics attempt a reconciliation of autonomy and independence?

chapter six

Igbo metaphysics in retrospect

At the beginning of part two, our main section on Igbo metaphysics, we noted that traditional metaphysics as a search for ultimate meaning seeks a description and identification of the intelligible nature, structure and characteristic qualities of reality. Because metaphysics is primarily concerned with the inquiry into ultimate principles, this traditional metaphysics tends to be immediately theoretical rather than practical. Since its distinctive feature is the comprehensiveness of its questions, it forms the background for our more restricted, everyday concerns.

In the preceding chapters an effort has been made to tease out a metaphysics from the language, culture, and socio-religious life of a people, the Igbos, whom we described in our introductory chapter as being more practically than theoretically oriented. For them the principal meanings according to which they live their practical daily lives are those they have extracted from their environment. Their thoughts are part and parcel of their practical and symbolic views of the world around them. Because their philosophy is closely tied to their practical way of life, they hardly engage in the kind of theoretical thinking characteristic of, or associated with, traditional metaphysics. This is the problem that Igbo metaphysics has been encountering throughout this work: Igbo thought trying to formulate a metaphysics out of the practical and symbolic views gathered from the Igbo life experience. Igbo culture has not suffered the pangs of the philosophical and religious controversies of the Western world in which modern philosophy came to birth in a criticism of religion.

Hence Igbo thought has not been exposed to those circumstances that have called for certain kinds of rationalism.

But does the fact that Igbo thought at present lacks a systematic formulation of the Western kind mean that the Igbos have no metaphysics? The answer is no, for the following reason: the preceding chapters have shown that the Igbos do not lack a description and identification of the intelligible nature, structure, and characteristic qualities implied in their cultural milieu. Their metaphysics from a Western viewpoint might be called implicit because it has not been organized as a formal system. But it remains, nonetheless, a framework of their experience of life, and thus continues to structure their culture and their language.

At this juncture a pertinent question to ask is: do we have in this study a metaphysics as done by an Igbo, or an Igbo metaphysics? In other words, is there such a thing as an Igbo metaphysics as there is, for instance, Greek or German metaphysics? I hereby state categorically that there is such a thing as an Igbo metaphysics. What we have done in this work is nothing but a pioneer's attempt at a formal articulation of an Igbo metaphysics. It is not a metaphysics as done by an Igbo. What is metaphysics if not one's God–man–world conceptual scheme or relationship; how one understands and interprets this scheme; what this scheme means to one, and how one's being, life and existence are determined by the relationship involved. In the preceding pages we have seen nothing but an articulated form of the Igbo concept of this God–man–world relationship. The Igbos understand and interpret this relationship in a way specific to them. In chapter three, for example, the Igbo mentality did not require any outside indoctrination to arrive at the fact that everything in the material universe has a beginning in the world of the unseen.[1] The Igbos show this in the mythical story of the origin of fire which we saw in chapter three.

The key to the Igbo understanding and interpretation of life and existence, beings and Being is given to us in chapter four. Here the Igbo mentality opens up the question of Being from the Igbo notion of man as *mma-di*, the "good that is." This gives the Igbo mind the clue to a general notion of Being as "good that is" because of having been created by Chineke. A closer study of Chineke reveals that He is the ultimate source of being, life, and existence, and yet He is Chi-ukwu, the almighty. So the Igbo mentality has its own unique way of understanding the God–man–world scheme: All things including man are "goods that are" because they are created by God who is Chineke, Osebuluwa, and Chi-ukwu. In this respect there must be such a thing as Igbo metaphysics, and since it is this Igbo way of understanding the God–man–world relationship that is articulated in the preceding pages, it is correct to say that what we have in this work is an Igbo metaphysics.

Furthermore, a scrutiny of what can actually be called metaphysics reveals that metaphysics is not a doctrine. Rather, metaphysics is a manner of questioning. What we have seen in this work can never be rightly construed as a doctrine, for it is not handing to its readers any form of belief. It is an articulated form of questioning. It is the Igbo manner of questioning with respect to the meaning of reality, being, life, and existence. In the face of the mysteries of life that surround him, the Igbo begins to wonder: What does it mean to be? A clue to the answer comes from the Igbo notion of man as mma-di (good that is). To be is to be the "good that is." Why would beings be the "goods that are?" Here the Igbo questioning mind arrives at the fact that beings are the "goods that are" because they are created by God who is Chi-na-eke, Ose-bulu-uwa, and Chi-ukwu. The meaning of reality is thus discovered in an Igbo way: God is the meaning of reality, for he is the ultimate source and end of being. Man is created to be free and yet dependent on his creator. The whole universe has a purpose for its creation and is guided by God to the fulfillment of this purpose. All this is the manner of Igbo questioning which is strictly metaphysical. This is what we have seen articulated in this work. Therefore this work is an Igbo metaphysics.

All the notions developed in this work are used by the Igbos, of course, not in English but in the Igbo language. My readers may tend to question whether these notions are really Igbo because some of them are similar to the Western metaphysical notions. For example, the Igbo notion of God as Osebuluwa is similar to the Western notion of divine providence.

My response to this is twofold: first, the Igbo metaphysical notions developed in this work may be similar to their corresponding notions in Western metaphysics but they are, in most cases, not exactly the same. They may appear to be the same simply because of language. For one to express an Igbo notion in a way it will be fairly intelligible to the Western reader, one is compelled to employ the nearest English terms. For example, take the notions mentioned above, osebuluwa and divine providence. For Westerners the notion of divine providence emphasizes the idea of God planning and caring for the creatures. The Igbo notion of Osebuluwa emphasizes the idea of carrying (bulu). So for the Igbos God is seen not only as planning and caring for creatures but even as carrying them. In Western culture human beings don't usually carry things on themselves, rather they pull them or push them. But in the Igbo culture there is a lot of carrying by individuals. For instance, a mother is always seen carrying her baby on herself and not pushing or pulling the baby in a cart. On account of these types of variations in the Igbo and Western cultures, it is difficult for the Westerner to comprehend what the Igbo means exactly by God carrying (bulu) creatures. This shows that even those Igbo notions we expressed in English as similar to Western notions may still be different in meaning for the Igbos. Hence it is wrong to maintain, as some of my readers may be tempted to, that the notions we have developed in this work are not originally Igbo, but are influenced by the Western metaphysics.

The second part of my response is that the fact that a notion developed in Igbo metaphysics corresponds to a Western metaphysical notion does not necessarily mean that the Igbo notion cannot be equally original to the Igbos as that of Western metaphysics is to Westerners. It could simply mean that, according to an English proverb, "great minds think alike." What is found in the one culture could also be at home in another culture. The notions developed in this work are notions used by the Igbos. They are not arbitrarily introduced by the author. Therefore this work is nothing but an Igbo metaphysics. Hence there is such a thing as an Igbo metaphysics.

Surely, like the people of India who have never divorced religion from philosophy, the Igbos have not drawn a clear line between their religion and metaphysics. The Igbo search into the intelligibility of reality is part of the Igbo inquiry into fundamental religious questions such as: who are we? Whence do we come and whither are we going? What is the purpose of our having been created? This kind of inquiry is metaphysical, even though it is not expressed by the Igbos in a technical language similar to that used by philosophers of the West. Having come to birth in a criticism of religion, some forms of Western metaphysics can be the kind of rationalization of religious experience that "rationalizes away" rather than expresses this experience. But before Western metaphysics took this turn, it was in its Platonic form, a borrowing, as E. R. Dodds[2] has shown, of a religious framework of thought that was, ironically, used to criticize prevailing religious notions.

Igbo metaphysics, as we have depicted it, is implicit in the religious experience, the language, in the whole cultural milieu of the people. Accordingly, it does not set out to prove, for example, as did Aquinas, that theology is a science. Instead, it sets out a *Weltanschauung*: a religious, social and cultural way of life.

In these pages a move has been made in the direction of attempting a systematic formalization of this metaphysics. This is possible because of the harmony that exists between Igbo practical and theoretical views. Evidence of this is in my treatment of the Igbo notion of being in chapter four, and the Igbo knowledge of God as the ultimate cause of being in chapter five. Reasoning from the practical experience expressed in the Igbo name for man, I have attempted to develop a general notion of being. The symbolic views of God as he is experienced by the Igbo in his daily life and expressed in the names for God, provide us with a formulation of the Igbo understanding of being in its ultimate cause.

Igbo metaphysics thus presented should be a great asset to the future development of the various disciplines that make up the entire Igbo body of knowledge. Future Igbo thinkers should no longer be caught up in the initial problem of how and where to begin. For instance, to develop a system of Igbo moral thought, one has to draw, among others, from the Igbo ideas of the community of being, of man as a unity of soul and body, of God as Chi-na-eke, Ose-bulu-uwa, and Chi-ukwu, the ultimate source of being. Also the political philosophy of the Igbos should flow from the principles fundamental to the Igbo way of life. Such principles must be based on the concept of Igbos as a part of a community of being: living, thinking, and acting together for a purpose.

Today there is much talk about the Africanization of the African Church. For this to materialize it will certainly entail a systematic development of some elements of African theology. But African theology, to possess a truly African identity, must be deeply involved in African metaphysics, that is, in the African way of understanding man and God. But the idea of an African metaphysics will remain too peripheral, too much of a figment of the imagination, unless it is articulated by a particular people of Africa. It is hoped that the present effort at Igbo metaphysics will serve as a useful contribution to this end. Igbo metaphysics should lead not only to a further development of Igbo philosophy and theology, but could also serve as an incentive for evolving a formally articulated African philosophy and theology.

The particular aim of this work has been to show how the Igbos in their way of life and thought endeavor to grapple with the problem of the meaningfulness of the universe. The whole treatment of "being" has been an attempt to face this problem. The discussion of the Igbo language, culture, and socio-religious milieu provides a background for the Igbo way of thought. Elements from the history of philosophy have been brought in only to help us develop some Igbo ideas and discuss some of the issues they entail.

From this study one understands that there is more to the universe than appears at first glance. Questions about where the universe came from and where it is going, whether it has any kind of unity or not, who we are and where we are going: all these concern the meaning of reality. They ultimately find their answer in the affirmation of God as Chineke, the source of all being and the guiding force in its development.

There is a fundamental unity of being since all beings derive from God as their creator and participate in his being. We, as part of God's creation, share in the being and goodness of God. Thus the Igbos have a hierarchical view of the universe, with God as the source and destiny of being. We fit into the structure of being as those who are cared for and supported by God as Osebuluwa.

Even though our knowledge of the ultimate cause of being, God, is far from being a perfect knowledge, what we have seen in this work is that according to Igbo metaphysics, man can have a view of reality in which there is room for the acceptance of and beholdenness to God. In this respect Igbo metaphysics is an archetype of the rest of African philosophy. It moves in the direction of a proper affirmation of God.

This direction seems to be the logical consequence of the African way of life which has been described in the writings of anthropologists, sociologists and theologians as being deeply religious:

> African man lives in a religious universe. Both that world and practically all his activities in it are seen and experienced through religious understanding and meaning.[3]

Some of our contemporaries who are presently engaged in developing African philosophy may now see that an African philosophy of the kind presented in Igbo metaphysics can have a systematic religious orientation.

The Igbo metaphysical view of the world is compatible with the divine revelation at the heart of the Judeo-Christian religious tradition. "The role of metaphysics as a science," Jolivet has noted,

> is to enable us gradually to purify our ideas of divinity and, to understand, moreover, that God is par excellence the infinite "Beyond," the absolutely "Other."[4]

Yet, as we have seen, this "Beyond," this wholly "Other," is "chi," an actual presence, immediately at hand as the ground of one's being. By means of his creative action as Chi-na-eke, this wholly "Other" in some way dwells in each and every creature. Thus he is more present to all beings than they are to themselves.

> God is the act of all our moments, and if, insofar as the senses are concerned, he is nothing, it is precisely because he is everything.[5]

In the Igbo culture the creative presence of God is so much a part of daily existence that the need does not arise for a possible verification. Concepts like Chi, Chi-na-eke, Ose-bulu-uwa, and the other ideas expressed in Igbo names, are all expressions of the living presence and activities of God.

Igbo metaphysics thus presented does not, of course, boast of having answers to all the questions about being. It has its own weaknesses. For instance, we have seen that the Igbo theory of duality is up against the problem of universals which it makes no effort to resolve. A possible objection to Igbo metaphysics is that it derives from a culture limited to a purely ethnic perspective, a culture that is not heterogeneous like Western culture. Granted this fact, the question then is: Can Igbo culture really stand up to the challenge of other cultures, especially to that of "the West" which for various historical reasons has achieved a position of economic and political dominance? Because of this position of preeminence, Western institutions, intellectual and religious as well as social and political, have achieved an unprecedented éclat. In the light of this, are there elements in Igbo culture that have transcultural validity? Or is Igbo culture simply a tribal culture of little or no relevance to other points of view?

As Igbo society stands today, there are no clearcut answers to these questions. Igbo society, like that of most African people, is going through a period of modernization: a period of transition from the purely traditional to one that is a blend of the traditional and alien values that must be accommodated because the Igbos are also part of our global society. As might be expected, these alien values must be designated such because they are in conflict with what is traditional. This situation is clearly depicted by Chinua Achebe in his portrayal of the characters of Okonkwo and Obierika in his novel, *Things Fall Apart*. In a scene that depicts the settling of the early missionaries and colonizers in Igboland, Okonkwo, the upholder of tradition, was eager to drive them out of the village of Umuofia. But Obierika says:

> It is already too late. . . . Our men and our sons have joined the ranks of the stranger. They have joined his religion and they help to uphold his government. . . . Now he (the stranger) has won our brothers, and our clan can no longer act like one. He has put a knife on the things that held us together and we have fallen apart.[6]

For most Africans, the first reaction to foreign influences was to reject them. African societies value their traditions and are unwilling to pay the price of losing them. But is the encounter with other values necessarily deleterious? A good number of Igbo communities have openly welcomed and adjusted to this "culture shock." Obviously there are other communities that would prefer not to compromise. They cannot envisage an enrichment of the traditional by any outside forces. It has not been the purpose of this work to pose the question directly: Can the Igbo culture as it is presented to us in its metaphysics maintain its viability in the age of technology? Since this question carries us far beyond the scope of this study—for it engages us in both anthropology and sociology—it suffices to point it out here as food for thought.

Christianity came to the Igboland about a hundred and fifty years ago (1841–1983). As one might expect, it met with opposition from the traditional society. It was during this same period that the colonial administration forced itself upon the people of Nigeria. The missionaries who ushered in the Christian faith did much good. However, some initial mistakes were made. One of these mistakes was the imposition of a foreign culture on the people. Three forces were in operation against the established traditional norms and conventions. The missionaries, the colonial trading companies, and British administration literally imported their Western culture and superimposed them on the traditional culture. Worse still, these agents tended to obliterate all that was traditional. Elements in the traditional culture not found in the foreign culture were labeled as devilish and uncivilized: they were earmarked for annihilation or replacement with the "superior, civilized, and saintly" elements of the foreign culture. It was good to introduce Christianity, civilization, and modern methods of trading, but it was necessary to allow the people to assimilate the new values into their own cultural values without brainwashing them into believing that nothing in their culture was good.

The inevitable result of the imposition of the imported culture on the Igbos, as on all other African peoples, was that a protracted series of conflicts and confusion accompanied the change in the way of life of the people as they struggled to assimilate the new values. The effect of the change was described by E. Obiechina thus:

> The first impact of change undermined collective solidarity and the traditional and therefore the ideological matrix that held the pre-colonial traditional society together. The introduction of Christianity, for instance, alienated the converts from their traditional loyalty to the ancestors and with that went, for them at any rate, the strongest sanction for individual action, social attitudes and behavior. The collective conscience was split and the community could no longer speak with one voice.[7]

The traditional life was characterized by the collective solidarity of people who shared common customs and beliefs, were linked by blood or marriage ties, and had, above all, an identical world view. As Obiechina correctly indicated, Christianity initially militated against the collective solidarity of the people, for the early Christian converts neither appealed to clan solidarity nor responded to its appeal. The neophytes tended to segregate themselves from the non-initiates.

It is important to note that this polarization between the neophytes and the traditionalists was well pronounced due to what we referred to as the initial mistakes of the early missionaries, namely, the condemnation of the people's culture and the imposition of an alien culture. The traditional communities were hardly given the chance to assimilate the new ideologies of the Christian faith into the traditional culture. No sooner did the Christians come to a place than they began actively to destroy the religious, and therefore ideological foundation of the society. This state of affairs could have greatly affected the metaphysical mentality of the Igbos were it not for the fact that an imposed culture never lasts. Its time is always short-lived. As soon as the Christian faith had taken root in Igboland and when Nigeria had gained her independence from Britain, the truth surfaced without delay. In both political and religious circles people began to realize that politics and Christianity do not necessarily mean a destruction of the people's original sense of values. Indigenous theologians sought to establish a common ground between Christianity and the traditional life of the people. Consequently, both the Christians and the non-Christians began to reunite and restore their collective responsibility and identical worldview.

Thus one can rightly say that the metaphysical mentality of the Igbos has not been basically altered either by colonization or by the introduction of Christianity. The effects of Christianity on the Igbo metaphysics can be seen only in our language and method of articulation. Because I was educated by the missionaries, my language of articulation is that of the missionaries, English. For the work to be intelligible to Western readers, my method of articulation could not be that of the Igbos. It had to be in accord with Western understanding. Hence I adopted analysis and interpretation as my method of articulation. These effects, evidently, do not concern the Igbo metaphysical mentality but its method of presentation.

The treatment of the contemporary problem of human freedom in this work has not been exhaustive.[8] As has been remarked in chapter five, this problem is not something new in philosophy. It is a perennial problem. But today it is attracting concern because of the tendency of this age to view man as the sole arbiter of meaning. The revolution that technological and biological breakthroughs have wrought has resulted in unprecedented changes in the way this age looks at man and his role in creation. Affluence and luxuries for a large portion of the human population, instant communication through electronic media via worldwide satellites, the preservation and prolongation of human life, the possibilities now being explored of artificially reproducing and modifying human life: the effects of all these have the tendency to make us believe that man is "everything" and is free to do everything.

Yet the ever present threat of the total destruction of the earth by man himself elicits a question mark concerning the wisdom involved in man's freedom. All this presents problems that call for an entirely different way of viewing man. Igbo metaphysics is saying that we should accept man as good within the context of creation. Creation concretizes man's relation to God. It is an affirmation of the mystery of man's dealing with God. We are called upon to help create the world—the fundamental work of God. Any achievement of man today, for example in technology, is ultimately that of God. Hence the freedom of man to invent and innovate is freedom within the creative providence of God.

Man, no matter how affluent, must be a creature. He is called by his creator to fulfill a purpose as a creature, to work for the fulfillment and not the destruction of God's plan and reason for creating man. Igbo metaphysics, in deriving a notion of being from man, is calling attention to man as that which is fundamental in philosophy. However, the attention is not to man in isolation, man as the sole arbiter of meaning and value, but to man as part of a totality of meaning. It is to man who recognizes his position as a finite entity whose personality is enriched and perfected by the "Other," the ultimate of which is God, Chi-ukwu. Thus in Igbo metaphysics we see the African mind as being holistic, giving a complete, rather than a truncated, view of man. Also in Igbo metaphysics we see how an African metaphysics must proceed from a deep consideration of the African culture, language, socio-religious milieu and above all a holistic view of the universe. We can understand the effort of post-reformation thinkers to separate philosophy from religious controversy. But as we know, this led to a hostile confrontation: a philosophy and science opposed to religion and a concept of man as absolute.

As I come to the end of this study, my retrospect comes out of my experience in the Igbo culture and also my background in Western philosophy. Born and brought up an Igbo and trained in Western metaphysics, I have my feet in both cultures. In the light of this fact, I dare to pose this question: What, to me, is distinctive of Igbo metaphysics in contrast to Western metaphysics?

The distinctive feature of Igbo metaphysics is that its notion of being is drawn from the concept of man and at the same time it is a theological metaphysics. It seeks a synthesis between anthropocentricism and theism. The man-centered concept of being is at the same time a religious view of reality with God as the ultimate source and man as a dependent entity. Here Igbo metaphysics offers a challenge to the still lingering concept of man introduced into Western thought by the rationalists of the modern period.[9] Igbo metaphysics has maintained the concept of human beings dependent upon God.

From what we have seen in this study it is improbable that Igbo thought will deviate from the direction it has already taken of maintaining man's beholdenness to God. In deriving the Igbo notion of being from a concept of man, Igbo metaphysics as a religious metaphysics is giving a witness to man as *homo religiosus*. The basis of this witness must be a belief in, an acknowledgement of, some personal Absolute Being. This belief or acknowledgement leads to an entire attitude of submission and respect to the supreme Being, God. Therefore Igbo metaphysics in its distinctive feature is, as it were, designed to uphold man's beholdenness to God rather than proclaim man as the rational absolute. The ground for this conclusion becomes obvious when we recall our indication in the introductory chapter that Igbo thought is closely tied to the people's practical rather than theoretical way of life. The Igbos would more readily understand the idea of man's dependence on "Our God" (Chi-ukwu Anyi), God who is actively present among us, the one whom we can conceive of and speak of in an anthropocentric manner, than they would understand the idea of a rational absolute which, in the last analysis, can be seen as the product of highly abstractive thinking.

This point clarifies the type of formalization involved in this study. When I indicated in the introduction that I was going to offer a formal presentation of Igbo metaphysics, the "outsider" may have supposed that I was going to offer a formalization that presupposed a rationalism akin, perhaps, to Aristotle's that led to his division of the sciences. It was such a rationalism that Saint Augustine identified as the way of the philosophers in contrast to "our" Christian way: a rationalism that subsequently called forth Aquinas's new synthesis. The formalization of Igbo metaphysics cannot be conceived in these theoretical patterns because we are dealing with a practical-theoretical science in the sense that, by nature, Igbo metaphysics is a lived philosophy rather than a purely theoretical or scientific enterprise. Hence my formalization consists in drawing out a rationalization of the lived experience of the people.

To capture and present what is truly an African way of viewing life and existence, beings and Being, one has to come to grips with the interplay of thought and action. For this reason some people are reluctant to speak of African philosophy. They think of philosophy in terms of a once fashionable Western model: an objective, abstract science. But for the African, philosophy is the way of life expressed in a people's rituals, language, and other cultural manifestations. Philosophy of this kind offers other peoples an ideal of human existance; specifically, an ideal of human dignity based upon the belief that all beings created by God are ontologically good and deserving of respect. The African principle of being one's brother's keeper is not simply a remnant of tribal society. Rather, the attentive mind will discern in it a reflection of that God–man–world scheme which we have presented in this work as Igbo metaphysics.

General Questions

1. Indicate the major problem of Igbo metaphysics and discuss it in the light of the traditional Western metaphysics.

2. Show how and why the Igbos, like the Indians, have not drawn a clear line of demarcation between their religion and metaphysics. Use samples from the text.

3. Discuss the importance of Igbo metaphysics in relation to:
   (a) the multifaceted disciplines of the entire Igbo body of knowledge;
   (b) African metaphysics in particular and philosophy in general;
   (c) African theology.

4. Show how:
   (a) Igbo metaphysics is an archetype of African philosophy;
   (b) Igbo metaphysical view of the world is compatible with the divine revelation.

5. Why is the perennial problem of human freedom attracting concern today? Highlight the merits of the Igbo metaphysical position on this problem.

6. Evaluate the distinctive feature of Igbo metaphysics in contrast to Western metaphysics; and present a justification of the kind of formalization involved in this study.

7. Is there such a thing as an Igbo metaphysics as there is, for instance, a Greek or German metaphysics? Draw arguments from the text in support of your position.

8. "For the African, philosophy is the way of life expressed in a people's rituals, language, and other cultural manifestations." What is the value of such a philosophy to humanity?

Appendices

Appendices

appendix one

A Way of handling the Igbo problem of the universals with some Western categories

Here is a possible interpretation of Igbo theory of duality as a way of handling the problem of the universals in the light of some Western categories.

If we accept that the theory of duality is a way of handling the problem of universals, two critical questions come to the fore. First, how can we account for the "act of respect to the unseen element" paid by the farmer? Second, from the theory of duality to what extent can we determine the Igbo idea of the universal?

The act of respect to the unseen element is verbalized by the farmer thus: "Eze ji, amaro m ụma kwụlia gi." that is, "King of yams, I did not willfully break you." A critical reflection on this sentence by a person conversant with the Igbo language will reveal that the phrase "Eze ji" (King of yams) is used metaphorically here. The broken pieces of yam before the farmer are really not the king of yams (they might even be the most ignoble parts of yam). The phrase is used to refer to the hidden reality of the yam, its essence, the foundation of the particular object. Therefore the "act of respect to the unseen element" should be understood as the act of respect to the essence of the yam. By act of respect, I mean the Igbo way of referring to the invisible self of the yam.

This brings us to a much more difficult question of determining the Igbo idea of the universal from the theory of duality. Reflecting on this theory one could find it hard to see how it could possibly lead to a defined Igbo idea of the universal. But a glimmer of light comes when we consider the theory as demonstrated in the Igbo cultural way of handling material things, for instance, the farmer making reference to the invisible element contained in the visible yam. Even in this case a possible way of construing the Igbo idea of the universal is to go to the extreme of regarding it as conceptualism or nominalism. A conceptualistic notion would propose that the invisible element in the material object for the Igbos is but a construct of the mind. Therefore the universals or the essences for the Igbos are thoughts or ideas in and constructed by the mind.

A nominalistic tendency in the tradition of scholastic philosophy would think that the reference to the invisible element is a way of recognizing only the individual object (yam) and not the features common to objects of the same class. This view finds its support in the Igbo language that has words such as "ji" (yam), nkita (dog), but has few one word abstract universals such as yamhood or doghood.

The Igbo idea of universals should best be understood in terms of the Western idea of realism: the invisible elements in any material object are equally as real as the visible aspects of the same object. If the former were simply the construct of the mind, the theory of duality would not be a deeper understanding of the existence of two worlds. In fact a reduction of the invisible element to a mere construct of the mind would be tantamount to a denial of the existence of two worlds. But, as we have seen in chapter three, the existence of two worlds is an accepted fact among the Igbos. Therefore, for them the invisible element in a material object is real. Granted this, we can conclude that the Igbo idea of the universal is a re-echo of the Western idea of realism according to which the reality is not just a construct of the mind. This conclusion, of course, is not without its problem when one comes to define the type of realism in question here, Platonic or Aristotelian.

From what we know of the Igbo theory of duality, that the invisible element, for example, in the yam, is regarded by the farmer as having its existence in the land of the unseen would indicate that for the Igbos universals are treated as objects separate from their instances. This can lead us to believe that the Igbos favor Platonic realism.

But as we stated in chapter three, the visible element exists only in combination with the invisible which cannot be construed as existing without the visible. This is obviously an inclination towards Aristotelian realism. Thus an ambiguity is involved. The reconciliation between the inclinations of Igbo metaphysics towards these two types of realism remains part of the perennial problem of the universals which calls for deeper and further investigation.

No doubt the way we have tried to handle this issue may present some problems to the Western reader who may think that we have imposed Western categories on Igbo thought. But this is the best that can be done given the present state of Igbo metaphysics. The merit of our treatment of the issue in this form is that it may generate a clue for further thinking on the part of Igbo philosophers. If the latter disagree with our interpretations, their disagreement may aid them to straighten out the problem and thus make positive contributions.

appendix two

Freedom and determinism

It is pertinent to note that an important issue consequent on our acceptance of God as Ose-bu-uwa is that of freedom and determinism. If God has a knowing plan for all creatures and directs them to this end, does it mean that he has already determined His creatures to follow His plan? If so, how could any creatures be said to be free in their actions? In other words, if God's activity embraces the height, depth, and breadth of created reality, is there any place for a finite activity which belongs to the being from which it comes? Or is it God rather than man, in the case of human activity, who acts as the center of man's being?

While we cannot enter the debate between thinkers down the ages, it does not hurt to mention the highlights. Two extreme positions can be identified on this: that of the deists who practically exclude God from the world; and that of the occasionalists who deprive man of all causal influence.

In the deist camp are people like Voltaire who profess to believe in God and accepts him as the cause of order but want to have enough room for human free will to operate.[1] For him God should stay in heaven and leave the world to men and to natural forces. Also David Hume, even though he rejected the deists' proof for God's existence and denied a free will in man,[2] he has a deistic notion of God. For him God is an omnipotent mind whose omnipotence is not wholly effective because reason which is founded on the nature of things, has a standard "external and inflexible even by the will of the Supreme Being."[3]

The modern scientific thought has followed this trend and attempted to banish God and freedom from the world. Thus as Alexandre Koyré put it:

> Newton had a God who 'ran' the universe according to his free will and decision, (but) the Divine Artifex had . . . less and less to do in the world. He did not even need to conserve it, as the world, more and more, became able to dispense with this service. Thus the mighty energetic God of Newton . . . became in quick succession, a conservative power, an *intelligentia supra-mundana*, a "*Dieu fainéant*" . . . The infinite Universe of the New Cosmology . . . inherited all the ontological attributes of divinity.[4]

In brief, the modern scientific thought suppressed the causality of God. Without going into any kind of discussion of this we simply note that this mentality militates against a knowledge of God—as Chi-na-eke who is actively present in all His creatures and whose presence means care and support for His creatures.

The occasionalists, for example, Malebranche and his Cartesian followers,[5] eager to preserve the primacy of God, went to the other extreme and conceived God's infinite causality in such a way that they emptied finite being of all causal effectiveness. According to them, God does everything. When, for instance, the teacher writing on the board moves the chalk it is actually God who moves it on the occasion of the teacher's willing to move it.

Both the deists and the occasionalists cannot give any satisfactory explanation of human freedom because both accept basic determinism either by God or by natural physical laws. In fact, with the expansion of modern science, it has become even increasingly difficult for philosophers to find any place for human freedom. Apparently man has become a hostage in the evolution of the universe, bound by its laws as the solar system is bound by the laws of motion. The picture of this attitude is well painted by Martin Buber:

> The quasi-biological and quasi-historical thought of today . . . have worked together to establish a more tenacious and oppressive belief in fate than has ever before existed. The might of the stars no longer controls inevitably the lot of man; many powers claim mastery, but rightly considered most of our contemporaries believe in a mixture of them. . . . This is made easier by the nature of the claim. Whether it is the 'law of life' of a universal struggle in which all must take part or renounce life, or the 'law of the soul' which completely builds up the psychical person from innate habitual instincts, or the 'social law' of an irresistible social process to which will and consciousness may only be accompaniments, or the 'cultural law' of an unchangeably uniform coming and going of histori-

cal structures . . . it always means that man is set in the frame of an inescapable happening that he cannot, or can only in his frenzy, resist.[6]

In reaction to the difficulty of placing human freedom many philosophers today can now admit a common-sense type of freedom without having to justify it metaphysically.

The fears expressed by some moral philosophers that the advance of the natural sciences diminishes the field within which the moral virtues can be exercised rests on the assumption that there is some contradiction in saying that one and the same occurrence is governed both by mechanical laws and by moral principles.

* * *

Not only is there plenty of room for purpose where everything is governed by mechanical laws, but there would be no place for purpose if things were not so governed.[7]

Morris Ginsberg, writing in an ethical context has the same approach:

The freedom that is required as a minimum condition of moral accountability is the ability to make an impartial estimate of the relative worth of the alternatives open to me and of acting accordingly. If I am not capable of any measure of impartiality, if I am unable to know what I am doing, or whether what I am doing is right or wrong, or again if having such knowledge I have not the emotional or cognitive energy to act in accordance with it, then I am neither free nor responsible.[8]

A clear solution to the problem of freedom can hardly be found. However, there are two alternatives. The first is to reject the reality of freedom. Should we do this, then we have to join the determinists and say that there is no paradox of divine and human causality. The second alternative is to accept the reality of freedom and then attempt to solve the paradox. A possible way of solving the paradox is to demonstrate that the affirmation of both divine and human causality is not a contradiction.

If, as we have shown, God is Chukwu, the Absolute Being, and He is Chineke, the source of all being, He is also the cause of all things. No explanation of anything in finite reality whatever can come outside of, or in spite of, the creative and providential causality of the Absolute Being. All causality and free activity can only be understood because of divine causality and never in spite of it.

We can therefore say that the relationship between divine causality and human freedom is that of cause and effect. Finite beings do actually exist. That means that they receive existence as their own and exist in themselves. If so, they should also receive activity as their own and act in themselves.

> If he has communicated his likeness, as far as actual being is concerned, to other things, by virtue of the fact that He has brought things into being, it follows that He has communicated to them His likeness, as far as acting is concerned, so that created things may also have their own actions.[9]

The key to the solution, one would say, is to realize that within the primary causality of God there can be secondary causality. The Absolute Being who is infinitely fruitful can, as Chi-na-eke in the power of His effective activity, create beings that are in turn productive. If, as Chi-ukwu, God has a power that is really unlimited, then it is not unreasonable to conclude that He can not only cause activities but also cause free activities regardless of how paradoxical they may appear to our limited minds.

With this brief consideration we may end by saying that the divine causality and human freedom are not contradictory to one another but meet in a paradox of cause and effect. This paradox is well explained in the words of Martin Buber:

> Destiny and freedom are solemnly promised to one another. Only the man who makes freedom real to himself meets destiny . . . destiny confronts him as the counterpart of his freedom. It is not his boundary, but his fulfillment; freedom and destiny are linked together in meaning.[10]

And Soren Kierkegaard[11] locates the mystery of freedom in God's omnipotence by saying that the greatest act that can be performed by any being, greater even than any end to which it can be created, is to make it free. To be able to do that omnipotence is necessary.

appendix three

Igbo orthography

A continual modification of Igbo orthography has been going on. As a result it is not easy to say which is the currently accepted orthography. However, for this study I have chosen to maintain the official orthography of 1961 with modifications as used in the 1979 reprinted third edition of *A Complete Course in Igbo Grammar*, by M. N. Okonkwo. My choice was due to the fact that the latter's work shows evidence of an up-to-date orthography since it has "the most modern research in Igbo grammar." It takes into consideration the research and conclusions reached by Igbo scholars, especially during the 1971, 1972, and 1975 seminars conducted jointly by the Department of African Studies and Extramural Studies, of the University of Nigeria, Nsukka, and the Society for the promotion of Igbo Language and Culture.

In the Igbo language there are eight vowels:

a ị ụ ọ · e i u o

These are classified under two main groups:

A GROUP: A Ị Ụ Ọ (that is, *A* plus three dotted vowels)
E GROUP: E I U O (that is, *E* plus three undotted vowels)

Key to Igbo pronunciations

Vowels:

A Group		
	A,a	is pronounced as in English Father
	I,i	is pronounced as in English It
	U,u	is pronounced as in English Uncle
	O,o	is pronounced as in English On
E Group	E,e	is pronounced as in English Measure
	I,i	is pronounced as in English In
	U,u	is pronounced as in English Food
	O,o	is pronounced as in English Oath

Consonants:

B, b	pronounced as in English Boy
D, d	pronounced as in English Dad
F, f	pronounced as in English Offer
G, g	pronounced as in English Gone
H, h	pronounced as in English Here
J, j	pronounced as in English Jump
K, k	pronounced as in English Keep
L, l	pronounced as in English Land
M, m	pronounced as in English Moment
N, n	pronounced as in English On
N̄, n	pronounced as in French Oui
P, p	pronounced as in English Pour
R, r	pronounced as in English Irregular
S, s	pronounced as in English Sunday
T, t	pronounced as in English At
V, v	pronounced as in English Victory
W, w	pronounced as in English We
Y, y	pronounced as in English my
Z, z	pronounced as in English Zone

Compounded Letters:

GB, gb	is treated as a syllabic nasal with *M* before the English *B*
CH, ch	is pronounced as in English Chair
Gh, gh	is pronounced as in German Brachte
KW, kw	is pronounced as in English Quiet
NY, ny	is pronounced as in English Eye
SH, sh	is pronounced as in English She
MM, mm	is pronounced as in English Swimming
NN, nn	is pronounced as in English Intention

Notes

General introduction

1. Robert W. July, *A History of the African People*, 2nd ed. (New York: Charles Scribner & Sons, 1974).

2. See the map showing all the countries in Africa, page 3.

3. July, *History*, 4.

4. These plateaus include the Jos Plateau in Nigeria, the Futa Jalon in Guinea, and Mount Tahat in the Ahaggar region of southern Algeria.

5. See Arthur N. Cook, *Africa: Past and Present* (London: Little-field, 1969), 21, and July, *History*, 9-13.

6. Cook, *Africa*, 21.

7. July, *History*, 9.

8. Western Sudan refers to all the areas from the modern Sudan through all West African countries up to Morocco in north western Africa.

9. Nigeria has more than 200 ethnic groups differing in language and culture.

10. See the map of Igboland on page 4.

11. Cyril Rex Niven, quoted by S. N. Nwabara, *Iboland: A Century of Contact with Britain 1860-1960* (London: Hodder and Stoughton, 1977), 17.

12. Arthur G. Leonard, *The Lower Niger and Its Tribes* (London: Frank Cass, 1968), 35.

13. N. W. Thomas, *Anthropological Report on Ibo-speaking Peoples of Nigeria*, vol. 4: *Law and Custom of the Asaba District of Southern Nigeria* (London: Harrison, 1914), 3-5.

14. Nwabara, *Iboland*, 18.

15. Nwabara, *Iboland*, 19. See also Frank Hives, *Juju and Justice in Nigeria* (London: John Lane, 1930), 248-52.

16. Thürsten C. Shaw, *Bronzes from Eastern Nigeria, Excavations at Igbo-Ukwu* (Eastern Nigeria, 1961), 162-65.

17. The Nri culture is that belonging specifically to a section of the Igbos regarded as a priestly class.

18. Onwuejeogwu, "An Ethno-historical Survey of the Ibo West and East of the Lower Nigerian Basin," (unpublished M.A. thesis), quoted by C. Obiego in "Igbo Idea of Life and Death in Relation to the Christian God," (Ph.D. diss., Pontifical Urban University, Rome, 1971), 3-8.

19. P. O. Achebe, "The Socio-Religious Significance of the Igbo Prenatal, Natal, and Puberty Rites," (Ph.D. diss., University of Innbruck, 1972.

20. M. C. English, *An Outline of Nigerian History* (London: Longmans, 1959), 6.

21. Niven, *Short History of Nigeria*, 6.

22. Jones and Mulhall, "An Examination of the Physical Type of Certain Peoples of Southeastern Nigeria," *Journal of the Royal Anthropological Institute of Britain and Ireland* 79 (1949): 11-12.

23. Achebe, "Socio-religious Significance of Rites," 2.

24. Ifeanyi Nwafor, "The Ibo Man: an Enigma," *Renaissance* (Enugu, March 10, 1973): 13.

25. Forde and Jones, *The Ibo and Ibibio-speaking Peoples of Southeastern Nigeria* (London: International African Institute, 1950), 50.

chapter one The Empirical method

1. Emmanuel M. P. Edeh, "Ancestor-worship and Traditional Rites in Nkanu" (B. A. diss., Bigard Memorial Seminary, Enugu, 1976), 19. The Nkanu share beliefs with the Swazi in Swaziland. Dibias are the traditional priests.

2. Throughout the questionnaire, the last name is the identifier of the respondent.

3. *Chukwu, Agbalumuanyanwu,* and *Chineke* are among the various names strictly reserved for the Supreme Being.

4. See note 3 above.

5. See note 3 above.

6. Igo-ini is an annual ritual of the Igbos in commemoration of the death of their ancestors.

chapter two The Igbo language, culture, and socio-religious milieu

1. See the appendix on Igbo orthography, 167.

2. E. Obiechina, *Culture, Tradition and Society in the West African Novel* (Cambridge: Cambridge University Press, 1975), 161.

3. In this ritual the host presents and shares a nut of kola with his guests. This is the conventional way of initial reception.

4. Obiechina, *Culture,* 165.

5. *Ibid.,* 156.

6. *Ibid.,* 157.

7. *Ibid.,* 16.

8. Pius Okpaloka, "The Supreme Being in Igbo Religion" (Unpublished report written at Enugu, Bigard Memorial Seminary, 1979), 28.

9. Obiechina, *Culture,* 202-03.

10. Basil Davidson, *The African Genius: An Introduction to Social and Cultural History* (London: Longmans, Green, 1969), 95.

11. Dibia fraternities are the associations formed by the traditional priests.

12. Nwabara, *Iboland*, 27.

13. John Boston, "Shrines in Udi Division," *Nigeria*, 61 (1959): 159.

14. W. G. R. Horton, "God, Man and Land in a Northern Ibo Village Group" *Africa* 26 (Jan. 1956): 23.

15. Obiego, "Igbo Idea of Life," 39.

chapter three The Origin, structure, and purpose of the universe

1. This type of igǫ ǫfǫ is also known as *iwa oji ututu (breaking the morning kola).*

2. Chapter one, 41.

3. E. G. Parrinder, *African Traditional Religion* 2nd edition (London: S.P.C.K., 1962).

4. Note that the author does not say whether or not he believes in reincarnation.

5. Father Innocent I. Egbujie, an Igbo, is a professor of philosophy at Boston College, Chestnut Hill, Newton, Massachusetts, U.S.A. See "The Hermeneutics of the African Culture," (Ph.D. dissertation, Boston College, 1976), 107.

6. *Loc. cit.*

7. Amos Tutuloa, *My Life in the Bush of Ghosts* (New York: Grove Press, 1954).

8. Chinua Achebe, *Things Fall Apart*, (Greenwich, Conn.: Fawcett Publications, 1959), 84.

9. See Victor C. Uchendu, *The Igbo of South East Nigeria* (New York: Holt Rinehart and Winston, 1965), 11-12. C. Obiego, "Igbo Idea of Life and Death in Relation to Christian God," (Ph.D. dissertation, Pontifical Urban University *de Propaganda Fide*, 1971), 113-22. Also see Pius Okpaloka, "The Supreme Being in Igbo Religion," (unpublished report, Bigard Memorial Seminary, Enugu, 1979), p. 23.

Note that this theory is still in its rudimentary stage, and that we cannot pretend to answer every question that may arise in the mind of a Western reader.

10. Yam is one of the most common, yet most valued and respected, food items among the Igbos.

11. See the appendix on an Igbo approach to the problem of the universals.

12. Benedict O. Eboh, "The Concept of the Human Soul in Igbo Traditional Philosophy" (Excerpt from laureate dissertation at the Pontifical Gregorian University, Rome, 1973), 23.

13. The Western reader is in danger of reading pantheism into the Igbo idea of "chi" because "chi", as we shall see in chapter five, is found in God and in all beings.

14. The concept of "chi" will be developed further under the Igbo names of God, *Chineke* and *Chukwu*, in chapter five. Also, the problem of participation will be discussed there.

15. Eboh, *Concept*, 24.

16. *Nze* is originally the name of a type of semi-wild bird believed to be the visible expression or embodiment of the respected dead ancestors. It is through them that some of the inhabitants of Ani Muo come to feed from the sacrificial meals of the living.

17. Eboh, *loc. cit.*

18. Obiechina, *Culture*, 42.

19. Aristotle, *Metaphysics*, E 1, 1025b18-1026a29.

20. Aristotle, *Physics*, II 1, 192b8-193b6.

chapter four An Igbo understanding of being

1. "Among the Igbos names were and are not considered as mere tags to distinguish one thing or person from another. They are expressions of the nature and significance of that which they represent or stand for." Hence they very often bring out the mentality of the people with due respect to the historical and cultural situa-

tions of actual life. See I. P. Anozia, "The Religious Import of Igbo Names" (Ph.D. dissertation, Pontifical Urban University *de Propaganda Fide* Rome, 1968), 87.

2. *De Veritate*, 1, 1c.

3. Martin Heidegger, *Being and Time*, trans. John Macquarrie and Edward Robinson. (New York: Harper & Row, 1962) pp. 22-23.

4. Bernard Lonergan, *Insight: A Study of Human Understanding* (New York: Philosophical Library, 1956), 359-60.

5. ST I, q. 22, a. 2, obj. 2.

6. Chinua Achebe, *No Longer at Ease* (Greenwich, Conn: Fawcett, 1969), 123.

7. Egbujie, *Hermeneutic*, 172.

8. ST I, q. 48, 1 and 3.

9. Egbujie, *op. cit.*, 114-15.

10. *Ibid.*, 116. *No-where-ness* here is an Igbo metaphor for nothingness.

chapter five Being and God

1. Adesanya is a Yoruba. Yorubas are an ethnic group in the western part of Nigeria.

2. Janheinz Jahn, *Muntu* trans. by M. Greme. (New York, 1961), 96-97.

3. John A. Wilson, *Before Philosophy* (Baltimore, 1972) 40-46.

4. Innocent I. Egbujie, "The Hermeneutics of the African Traditional Culture" (Ph.D. diss. Boston College, 1976), 102.

5. *Ibid.*, 173.

6. *Chukwu* is not the only name for God among the Igbos. Among the other the other names are Chineke and Olisa.

7. "Among the Igbo names were and are not considered as mere

tags to distinguish one thing or person from another. They are expressions of the nature and significance of that which they represent or stand for." Obiego, "Igbo Idea," 76. Also see Anozia, "Religious Import of Igbo Names," 87.

8. For the Igbo this is obvious from the fact that each person's Chi is active and responsive to the circumstances of life. For example, when a person in difficulties calls on his or her Chi, there is usually a response in the form of a marked improvement in the person's situation.

9. C. K. Meek, *Law and Authority in a Nigerian Tribe* (Oxford, 1937), 20.

10. Obiego, "Igbo Idea," 93.

11. See S. N. Ezeanya, "God, Spirits and the Spiritual World" *Biblical Revelation and African Beliefs* (London, 1969) 39, and W. O'Donnell, "Religion and Morality among the Ibo of Southern Nigeria," *Primitive Man* 4 (1931), 54-60.

12. Uchendu, *The Igbos*, 95.

13. Percy A. Talbot, *Peoples of Southern Nigeria* (London: Frank Cass, 1961), 280.

14. Onuora Nzekwu, *Wand of Noble Wood* (New York: New American Library, 1961), 96.

15. Simon Okeke, "Priesthood Among the Igbos of Nigeroia Studied in the Light of the Catholic Priesthood" (Ph.D. diss., University of Innsbruck, 1967), 56.

16. Meek, *Law and Authority*, 55.

17. According to the Igbos, everything both animate and inanimate has chi. Sometimes chi in man is said to direct man's actions.

18. Obiego, *Igbo Idea*, 95.

19. Martin Buber, *I and Thou*, Walter Kaufman, trans. (New York: Charles Scribner & Sons, 1970), 110-11.

20. *Ndu* or *idi ndu* can be translated as *life* in the sense of existence.

21. Obiego, *Igbo Idea*, 96.

22. ST I, q. 8, 1.

23. J. O'Connell, "The Withdrawal of the High God in West African Religion: An Essay in Interpretation," *Man* 62 (1962): 109ff.

24. E. Bolgai Idowu, *God in Yoruban Belief* (Lagos: Federal Ministry of Information, 1963), 9.

25. The Igbo Catholic Catechism that was in use in the old Onitsha Province until the 1950s had a picture of Osebuluwa on the back cover: God in the person of Jesus Christ carried the world in one palm and blessed it with the other hand.
    During my field research I learned that this picture can be traced back to the early missionaries. Father Vogler, a missionary who worked on the first Igbo catechism, chose *Osebuluwa* rather than *Ony-nwe-anyi (He who owns us)* to translate Lord. The Catholic indigenous committee working on the catechism would not choose the other word because the Protestant religious books used it.
    When Father Shanahan went to Abuchi, he saw that the people represented a deity known to them as *Ose* as carrying and supporting the world on its back. He modified this symbolism for the portrayal of the Christian God.

26. Obiego, *Igbo Idea*, 95.

27. My expression is culled from my life with the Igbos.

28. Søren Kierkegaard, *Concluding Unscientific Postscript*, David F. Swanson and Walter Lowrie, trans. (Princeton: Princeton University Press, 1941), 220.

29. Robert L. Hurd, "The Concept of Freedom in Rahner," *Listening* 17 (1982): 140.

30. Hurd, *loc. cit.*

31. Hurd, *op. cit.*, 150.

32. Chinua Achebe, *No Longer At Ease* (Greenwich, Conn.: Fawcett Publications, 1960) 75-76.

33. *Ibid.*, pp. 81-82. Also see Egbujie, *Hermeneutic*, 189.

34. Egbujie, *op. cit.*, 190.

35. *Ibid.*, 191.

chapter six   Igbo metaphysics in retrospect

1. See above, 69-71.

2. E. R. Dodds, *The Greeks and the Irrational* (Berkeley and Los Angeles: University of California Press, 1966), 210.

3. John S. Mbiti, *African Religion and Philosophy* (New York: Doubleday Anchor Book, 1970), back cover.

4. Regis Jolivet, *Man and Metaphysics*, trans. B. M. G. Reardon (New York: Hawthorn Books, 1961), 111.

5. Ibid.

6. Achebe, *Things Fall Apart*, 157-58.

7. Obiechina, *Culture*, 219.

8. For a further development of this problem, see the appendix on freedom and determinism.

9. Here we refer to the Western philosophers like Feuerbach, Marx, Nietzsche and Sartre. For these thinkers, as we have indicated in chapter five, the human subject must seek birth through himself as absolute will-to-power, self-invention, and freedom. Following the same trend, modern scientific thought has attempted to banish God and freedom from the world. See Hurd, "Concepts", 150.

Also see Etienne Gilson and Thomas Langan, *Modern Philosophy: Descartes to Kant* (New York: Random House, 1963), 335. The deists, such as Thomas Jefferson, practically exclude God from the world.

Also see Alexandre Koyré, *From the Closed World to the Infinite Universe* (Baltimore: The Johns Hopkins Press, 1957), 276. The divine artifex became the *dieu faineant*, while the infinite universe inherited all the ontological attributes of divinity. See the appendix on free and determinism for more details.

appendix two   Freedom and determinism

1. Gilson and Langan, *Modern Philosophy*, 335.

2. Here Hume denies the freedom which would be experienced in an act which requires a reaching to the more profound levels of one's being in order to determine one's life. This is a self-determination which transcends external determinations and even the spontaneous inclinations that arise from within.

3. David Hume, *An Enquiry Concerning Human Understanding* ed. L. A. Selby-Bigge (Oxford: Clarendon Press, 1902), 40.
See also *A Treatise on Human Nature* ed. by L. A. Selby-Bigge (Oxford: Clarendon Press, 1896), 633 n.

4. Koyré, *From the Closed World*, 276.

5. Gilson and Langan, *Modern Philosophy*, 93-107.

6. Buber, *I and Thou*, 56.

7. Gilbert Ryle, *The Concept of Mind* (New York: Barnes and Noble, 1960), 80-81.

8. Morris Ginsberg, *On The Diversity of Morals* (New York: Macmillan, 1957), 81-82.

9. SCG III, c. 69, n. 14.

10. Buber, *I and Thou*, 53.

11. *The Journals of Søren Kierkegaard: A Selection* ed. and trans. by Alexander Dru (Oxford: Oxford University Press, 1938), 180-81.

Bibliography

Achebe, Chinua. *No Longer at Ease*. Greenwich, Conn.: Fawcett Publications, 1969.

_____. *Things Fall Apart*. Greenwich. Conn.: Fawcett Publications, 1959.

Anozia, I. P. "The Religious Import of Igbo Names." Ph.D. dissertation, Pontifical Urban University *de Propaganda Fide*. Rome, 1968.

Aquinas, St. Thomas. *Introduction to St. Thomas Aquinas*. Translated and edited by Anton C. Pegis. "Modern Library." New York: Random House, 1965.

Aristotle. *Basic Works*. Edited by Richard McKeon. New York: Random House, 1941.

Boston, John. "Shrines in Udi Division" in *Nigeria* 61 (1959).

Buber, Martin. *I and Thou*. Translated by Walter Kaufman. New York: Charles Scribner and Sons, 1970.

Cook, Arthur N. *Africa: Past and Present*. London: Littlefield, 1969.

Davidson,. Basil. *The African Genius: An Introduction to Social and Cultural History*. London: Longmans, Green, 1969.

Eboh, Benedict O. "The Concept of the Human Soul in Igbo Traditional Philosophy." Rome: Excerpt from Laureate dissertation in philosophy, Pontifical Gregorian University, Rome, 1973.

Edeh, Emmanuel M. P. "Ancestor Worship and Traditional Rites in Nkanu." B.A. Thesis in the Department of Theology of Bigard Memorial Seminary. Enugu, 1976.

Egbujie, Innocent I. "The Hermeneutics of the African Traditional Culture." Ph.D. dissertation, Boston College, 1976.

Ezeanya, S. N. "God, Spirit and the Spiritual World." in *Biblical Revelation and African Beliefs*. London: Lutherworth Press, 1969.

Gilson, Etienne and Thomas D. Langan, *Modern Philosophy: Descartes to Kant*. New York: Random House, 1963.

Ginsberg, Morris. *On The Diversity of Morals*. New York: Macmillan, 1957.

Heidegger, Martin. *Being and Time*. Translated by John Macquarrie and Edward Robinson. New York: Harper & Row, 1962.

Hives, Frank. *Juju and Justice in Nigeria*. London: John Lane, 1930.

Horton, W. G. R. "God, Man and Land in a Northern Ibo Village Group" *Africa* 1 (26 Jan. 1956).

Hume, David. *An Enquiry Concerning Human Understanding*. Edited by L. A. Selby-Bigge. Oxford: Clarendon Press, 1902.

_____. *Treatise on Human Nature*. Edited by L. A. Selby-Bigge. Oxford: Clarendon Press, 1896.

Idowu, E. Bolgi. *Olodumare: God in Yoruba Belief*. Lagos: Federal Ministry of Information, 1963.

Jahn, Janheinz. *Muntu*. Translated by M. Greme. New York: Grove Press.

July, Robert W. *A History of the African People*. 3rd ed. New York: Charles Scribner & Sons, 1984.

Kierkegaard, Søren. *Concluding Unscientific Postscript*. Translated by David F. Swenson and Walter Lowrie. Princeton: Princeton University Press, 1941.

_____. *The Journals of Søren Kierkegaard: A Selection*. Edited and translated by Alexander Dru. Oxford: Oxford University Press, 1938.

Koyré, Alexandre. *From the Closed World to the Infinite Universe.* Baltimore: Johns Hopkins Press, 1957.

Leonard, Arthur G. *The Lower Niger and Its Tribes.* London: Frank Cass, 1968.

Lonergan, Bernard J. *Insight: A Study of Human Understanding.* New York: Philosophical Library, 1956.

Mbiti, John S. *African Religions and Philosophy.* "An Anchor Book." New York: Doubleday, 1970.

Meek, Charles K. *Law and Authority in a Nigerian Tribe.* Oxford: Oxford University Press, 1937.

Niven, Cyril Rex. *A Short History of Nigeria.* London: Longmans, Green, and Co., 1952.

Nwabara, S. N. *Iboland: a Century of Contact with Britain 1860-1960.* London: Hodder and Stoughton, 1977

Nzekwu, Onuora. *Wand of Noble Wood.* New York: New American Library, 1961.

Obiechina, E. *Culture, Tradition and Society in the West African Novel.* Cambridge: Cambridge University Press, 1975.

Obiego, Cosmas. "Igbo Idea of Life and Death in Relation to Christian God." Ph.D. dissertation, Pontifical Urban University *de Propaganda Fide*, Rome. 1971.

O'Connell, J. "The Withdrawal of the High God in West African Religion: An Essay in Interpretation." *Man* 62 (1962): 109ff.

O'Donnell, W. "Religion and Morality among the Ibo of Southern Nigeria." *Primitive Man* 4 (1931): 54-60.

Okeke, Simon. "Priesthood Among the Igbos of Nigeria Studied in the Light of the Catholic Priesthood." Thesis, University of Innsbruck, 1967.

Okonkwo, M. N. *A Complete Course in Igbo Grammar.* 3rd ed. Onitsha: Macmillan Nigeria, 1979.

Okpaloka, P. "The Supreme Being in Igbo Religion." *Exercitatio Practica,* Bigard Memorial Seminary, Enugu, 1979.

Parrinder, Edward Geoffrey. *African Traditional Religion.* 2nd ed. London: S. P. C. K., 1962.

Ryle, Gilbert. *The Concept of Mind.* New York: Barnes and Noble, 1960.

Shaw, Thurstan C. *Igbo-ukwu: An Account of Archaeological Discoveries in Eastern Nigeria.* 2 vols. Evanston, Ill.: Northwestern University Press, 1970.

Talbot, Percy A. *Peoples of Southern Nigeria.* 2 vols. London: Frank Cass, 1969.

Thomas, Northcote W. *Law and Culture of the Asaba District,* 4th vol. of *Anthropological Report on Ibo-speaking Peopes of Nigeria.* 6 vols. London: Harrison, 1914.

Tutuola, Amos. *My Life in the Bush of Ghosts.* New York: Grove Press, 1954.

Uchendu, Victor C. *The Igbo of South East Nigeria.* New York: Holt Rinehart and Winston, 1965. "Case Studies in Cultural Anthropology."